You Can Play The Guitar

with Dan Morgan and Nick Penny

Illustrated by Mike Miller

CAROUSEL BOOKS
A DIVISION OF TRANSWORLD PUBLISHERS LIMITED

Other titles in the YOU CAN series include:

YOU CAN SWIM
YOU CAN BE A GYMNAST
YOU CAN PLAY FOOTBALL
YOU CAN PLAY CRICKET
YOU CAN RIDE
YOU CAN PLAY TENNIS
YOU CAN BE A BALLET DANCER

All published by CAROUSEL BOOKS

YOU CAN PLAY THE GUITAR
A CAROUSEL BOOK 0 552 542458

First published in Great Britain by Carousel Books

PRINTING HISTORY
Carousel edition published 1983

Carousel Books are published by
Transworld Publishers Ltd.,
Century House, 61–63 Uxbridge Road,
Ealing, London W5 5SA

Made and printed in Great Britain by
The Guernsey Press Co. Ltd.,
Channel Islands.

CONTENTS

RECOMMENDED BOOKS

GUITAR by Dan Morgan. Corgi Books. A comprehensive handbook which deals with all styles of guitar playing from basic chords to the reading of solo guitar pieces.

SPANISH GUITAR by Dan Morgan. Corgi Books. A basic guide to Finger Style playing including Classical, Flamenco, Jazz and Folk and Blues styles, including instruction in reading musical notation and tablature.

SOLO GUITAR PLAYING — Books 1 and 2 by Frederick M. Noad. Pub. Omnibus Press. These books are probably the most comprehensive available to the **serious** student of the Spanish Guitar. Book One contains sufficient material to enable a complete beginner to develop into a competent solo guitarist.

Book Two builds further on this foundation, with particular attention to Technique, Musicianship and Style. Both books offer a repertoire of Classical pieces and there is enough practice material to keep the beginner fruitfully occupied for at least three years. If you are really serious about the guitar and willing to work at it I don't think you could do better than buy these two books after you have worked your way through one, or both of the others.

There are of course many more books available and their number is growing every day, but those listed above will give you a good grounding without putting you to too much expense. This is particularly true in the case of the Corgi books, which are available at all good book stores and represent the best value on the market at the present time.

WHY PLAY THE GUITAR?

To answer the question above, it seems to me that probably the best reason for doing anything is that it's fun. Certainly that applies to playing the guitar. Nick Penny and I have both been playing for a large part of our lives — me rather longer because I'm more ancient — and yet every day we find that the guitar offers some new pleasure or satisfaction; the discovery of a new chord, a new piece of music, a new way of playing an old piece or some new adventure in sound that just happens when the instrument is there under our fingers. Neither of us would lay claim to being great players, but for each of us in our different way the guitar is an important part of our daily life.

For the sake of clarity Nick and I will speak with one voice throughout this book, so that mostly when the book says 'I' it really means 'we', because the matters involved have been discussed at length between us. The one exception to this rule is the chapter after this one, which is written by Nick from his own unique point of view as a guitar maker, a role upon which I, a mere player, do not feel qualified to intrude.

Like most things the guitar becomes more and more interesting and rewarding as you become more deeply involved. A prime illustration of this must be the Grand Old Man of the guitar, the Maestro Andres Segovia, who says: 'I was both my pupil and teacher, and I am learning still. It is better to be a pupil of an art at 90 than a master at 14.' That is his way of saying the same thing that I said in my first paragraph above. Playing the guitar is fun because there is always something more to learn however long you have been playing, which means that your knowledge is always growing and becoming more creative.

A remarkable thing about the guitar is the fact that looked at from the other end of the scale, from the point of view of an absolute beginner, those satisfactions and adventures commence from the very first time you pick up a guitar. Indeed, in my own case they began even before I actually handled the instrument, because I was fascinated by the appearance of the guitar. As a small boy, just looking at a guitar in a music shop window I somehow knew that it was going to play an important part in my life — a prediction which has long since been fulfilled.

You may find it difficult to believe, but although the guitar has been around in one form or another for centuries its present day popularity only began to explode into being about 25 years ago. Before that time, most youngsters with musical ambitions took up the saxophone or trumpet, because those were the instruments which dominated the popular music of the time.

Likewise in the classical field, the violin or piano were the most popular choices of instrument, with the guitar a very unlikely outsider, as Julian Bream, the great British guitarist, found out when he was a student at the Royal College of Music and it was suggested to him that for the sake of the reputation of that august establishment he *should take his guitar into the building by the back door*. The situation today is vastly

different, so that in addition to being the most widely played and popular instrument of all, the guitar is now recognised as holding a special position in the classical and concert fields.

Just why has the guitar become so popular? It seems to me that there are two main reasons. (1) Its portability and comparative fullness of sound, and (2) its adaptability. You can play the guitar anywhere and you can play almost any type of music you wish on it. That is to say, whether your interest lies in Classical music, Folk music, Blues, Rock and Roll, Flamenco or Jazz; any of these styles can be played on the guitar. There are several types of guitar, some of which are more suited than others for particular types of music, but they are basically the same instrument. We will discuss these different types of guitar later on.

Whatever your taste in music you will find that the guitar can help you to explore and enjoy it. You will also find that through playing the guitar you will begin to discover new and interesting types of music. What you play will be an expression of your own temperament, taste and ability. Your guitar will do as much or as little as you wish it to do for you. Its potential is all there awaiting only a reasonable amount of effort on your part to bring it into reality.

You may begin to wonder at this point just how much effort is involved in learning to play the guitar. The answer to that is, it's up to you. Nothing worthwhile is ever achieved without some effort, but there is no reason why the application of that effort should not also be a pleasure. Indeed, if you are to gain the right kind of satisfaction from your exploration of the guitar every moment of your playing should give you pleasure.

Whatever you do, don't make things unnecessarily hard for yourself by expecting too much all at once. Despite some of the irresponsible claims that have been made in the past **nobody ever learned to play the guitar in a day**. You will be able to make a pleasant sound on a guitar in only a few hours, because it is almost impossible to make a nasty one, but that does not mean that you will immediately be able to form your own Rock group or give your first solo concert. If you apply yourself in a regular routine — and routine is very important in anything of this nature as learning is a gradual process — your mind and fingers cannot fail to build up their knowledge of the guitar. On the other hand, if you try to do the whole thing at once you will only become tired and frustrated and end up getting nowhere.

At the beginning for instance, your fingers will become sore. It happens to all of us. At that point, don't go on forcing yourself to play, gritting your teeth against the pain. Better to retire gracefully and allow your finger ends to recover with a dab of surgical spirit to cool them down and help harden them. By the time you pick up the instrument again the soreness will have disappeared and your finger ends will already be on the way to developing those hard pads which are the mark of a guitarist.

So, before you start playing, bear these points in mind:

Take your time.

Be patient with yourself.

Develop a regular practice routine.

BUT ABOVE ALL HAVE FUN!

GUITAR IN THE MAKING

Can you remember how exciting it is to be given presents on Christmas Day? Well, the very best present I ever received was my first guitar. It was supposed to be a 'surprise' gift from my parents, but no amount of wrapping paper could disguise that tell-tale shape. And any doubt as to what it could be finally disappeared as I eagerly began unwrapping it. There was the muffled, but unmistakable twang of a guitar string — and we had played our first note together!

The most striking thing about this treasured new possession was the bright green tartan cover it came in, but it was not long before I began to discover new and exciting things about the guitar itself. It could make sounds of course, but it was also a beautiful object. It looked, felt, even **smelled**, unusual and interesting.

It was made of wood. The sides and back were a deep brown colour which shone with a gloss you could see your face in. The soundhole was surrounded by an intricate pattern of lines and squares in many colours. If you look at your own guitar you will find the same kinds of patterns and colours.

Another thing I discovered was how nice my guitar was to touch and hold. The neck and body were exquisitely carved and shaped so that they were quite smooth and rounded. I even took off the strings and gingerly felt about inside the soundhole. There seemed to be many more bits of wood glued in there, where no one could see them from the outside, some glued under the front itself. This was a real mystery to me. What possible use could they be if they couldn't be seen?

Now that I am involved in making and repairing guitars I know that there are many mysteries surrounding all musical instruments. You may not have thought about it, but there is something miraculous about how a fragile wooden box with strings across it can make any sound at all. More surprising still, one guitar may have a much lovelier sound than another, due to the way it is **made** rather than played. Two guitars may even look very much the same, but make quite a different sound.

I have already told you how my first guitar was made of a deep brown wood. It is with the wood that the story of how a guitar is made begins. The guitar maker, or **luthier**, as he is called by some people, after the lute maker of old, must select special timbers that are the pick of those grown all over the world. He may use **Mahogany** from Central America; **Rosewood** from Brazil or the East Indies; **Ebony** from Sri Lanka; **Spruce** from Central Europe or Canada. The woods used in a single guitar come from forests in several continents thousands of kilometres apart.

Despite this every piece of wood has one thing in common. Like you or I it **grew**. It started as the tiniest seed and spent many years being nourished by water and minerals taken by its roots from the earth around it. Think about the wood in your guitar. Even before being made into a guitar it has lived a long life among the sounds and activities of the forest, possibly for many hundreds of years in the case of a Spruce tree, and even when it has been made into a guitar the wood is still very much alive. It takes moisture from the air if the day is damp. It may appear to change colour from light to dark shades as you hold it up to the light. And, above all, it VIBRATES. It trembles into life whenever there is another sound in the same room. A guitar is so sensitive that if you just hold it while someone is speaking you may feel it vibrating in sympathy with the sound of their voice.

Luthiers have an interesting way of telling whether a piece of wood will make a good musical instrument. They will hold it at one end so that it hangs down with the other end free to swing about and give in a sharp rap with their knuckles. This will make the wood give off a ringing sound, rather like a distant church bell chiming. To the trained ear of the luthier the quality of sound given off by the wood in its raw state is a good indication as to the kind of sound it will bring to the guitar of which it forms a part.

Let's follow the luthier as he takes the wood into his workshop. This is a delightful place, full of the rich smells of fresh-sawn timber, glue, and various varnishes and polishes, each with its own aroma. Tools hang from the walls. There are saws and chisels in every possible shape and size.

There is even a tiny plane made of brass, called a **thumb plane**, which will take thin shavings from wood which needs specially delicate shaping. And there are all sorts of curiously shaped patterns and moulds, as well as parts of instruments at every stage of their making.

Guitars can be made from almost any type of wood, but certain woods have been found to give a much better sound and appearance than others. Our luthier uses Rosewood for the backs and sides of classical guitars, although cheaper models may use Mahogany. Every individual piece will differ slightly in thickness, but he will saw and plane Rosewood until it is about 2.5mm thick. If you check this with a ruler you will find that it is quite thin.

> To bend the sides into the shape that fits so snugly onto your thigh when playing, he first wets the wood, and then presses it against a specially heated pipe called a **bending iron**. He must be very careful, because the wood could easily break if pressed too hard. When the wood cools down again it still retains its new, curvy shape.

Where Rosewood is used for classical guitars, many luthiers use **Cypress** for Flamenco guitars. This is lighter in both weight and colour and gives the brighter sound more suited to Flamenco music. It also has a lovely smell, rather like lemons. In Spain,

Cypress trees grow mainly in cemeteries and the Spaniards with their own wry sense of humour call the Cypress a very sad tree.

A favourite wood among makers of steel-strung guitars is **Mahogany**. This may be planed slightly less thin, for the greater strength required in supporting steel strings.

The part of the guitar which has the most to do with how good it sounds is the front or **table**. Spruce or Cedar are most commonly used for this. They are light in colour, which is why there is often a contrast between the top and the back and sides of an instrument. The luthier has to use all his experience in deciding when the wood is thin enough to vibrate freely and give a good sound, whilst at the same time being thick enough to withstand the enormous pull of the strings. Since the pull on a guitar bridge may be over fifty kilos in tension, (equivalent to hanging a large sack of cement from such a delicate instrument) it is obvious that it must be well glued in place.

To strengthen the table the luthier also glues **bracing bars** on the **inside**. These are what my exploring hand felt when I put it through the soundhole of my first guitar. They are strips of wood which act rather like the frame of a kite or model aircraft, giving strength with a minimum of extra weight.

The bracing bars in a classical guitar are arranged in what is known as a **Fan** pattern, which was the design developed so effectively by the great Spanish luthier Torres. Inside most steel strung guitars there is a pattern called **Cross Strutting**. As you can probably guess from the names, one system uses a fan shape, while the other is based on a diagonal cross.

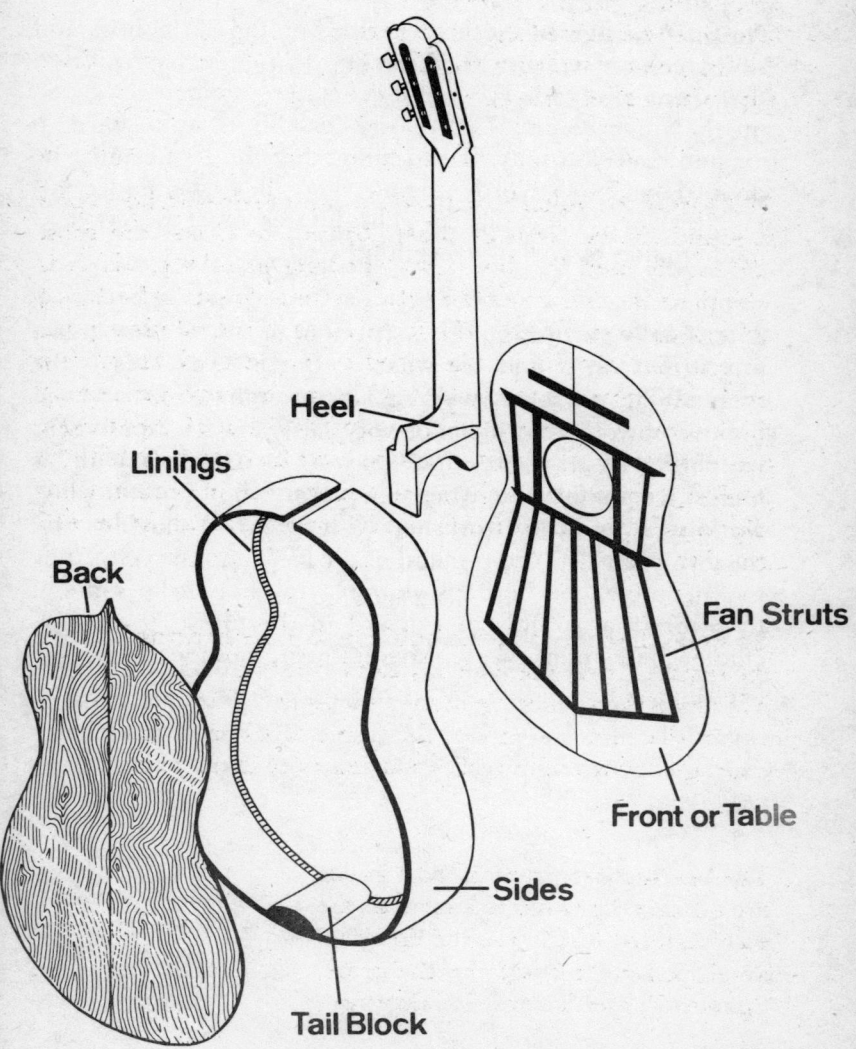

Heel

Linings

Back

Fan Struts

Front or Table

Sides

Tail Block

The **neck** is another of the vital parts of the instrument which must be made by the luthier to the best of his ability. This is usually made of Mahogany, and may be strengthened with a thin steel bar if steel strings are to be used. This is to prevent the neck warping or bending through being pulled constantly by the strings.

An Ebony **fingerboard** is then glued on top of the neck and silver bars or **frets** are inlaid across it. You may have noticed that these start wide apart and get closer together as they go up the fingerboard. The reason for this is quite hard to explain; but you may like to know that the string must be divided by 17.835 in order to find where the first and succeeding frets are to be placed. The luthier must be good at mathematics as well as everything else!

After finally varnishing the instrument the luthier can at last put strings on it and see what it sounds like. This is the moment he has been waiting for through weeks or even months of work, and it can be very satisfying for him to hear with his own ears the result of the work he has put in with his hands. Remember him when you pick up your guitar to play, working away in his workshop with the wood shavings and the lovely smells. And remember the trees and the years they took to grow . . . Perhaps your playing may echo some of those original sounds they heard in the forest; the happy chatter of the monkeys, or the soft murmur of the wind in the branches.

THE GUITAR AND ITS PARTS

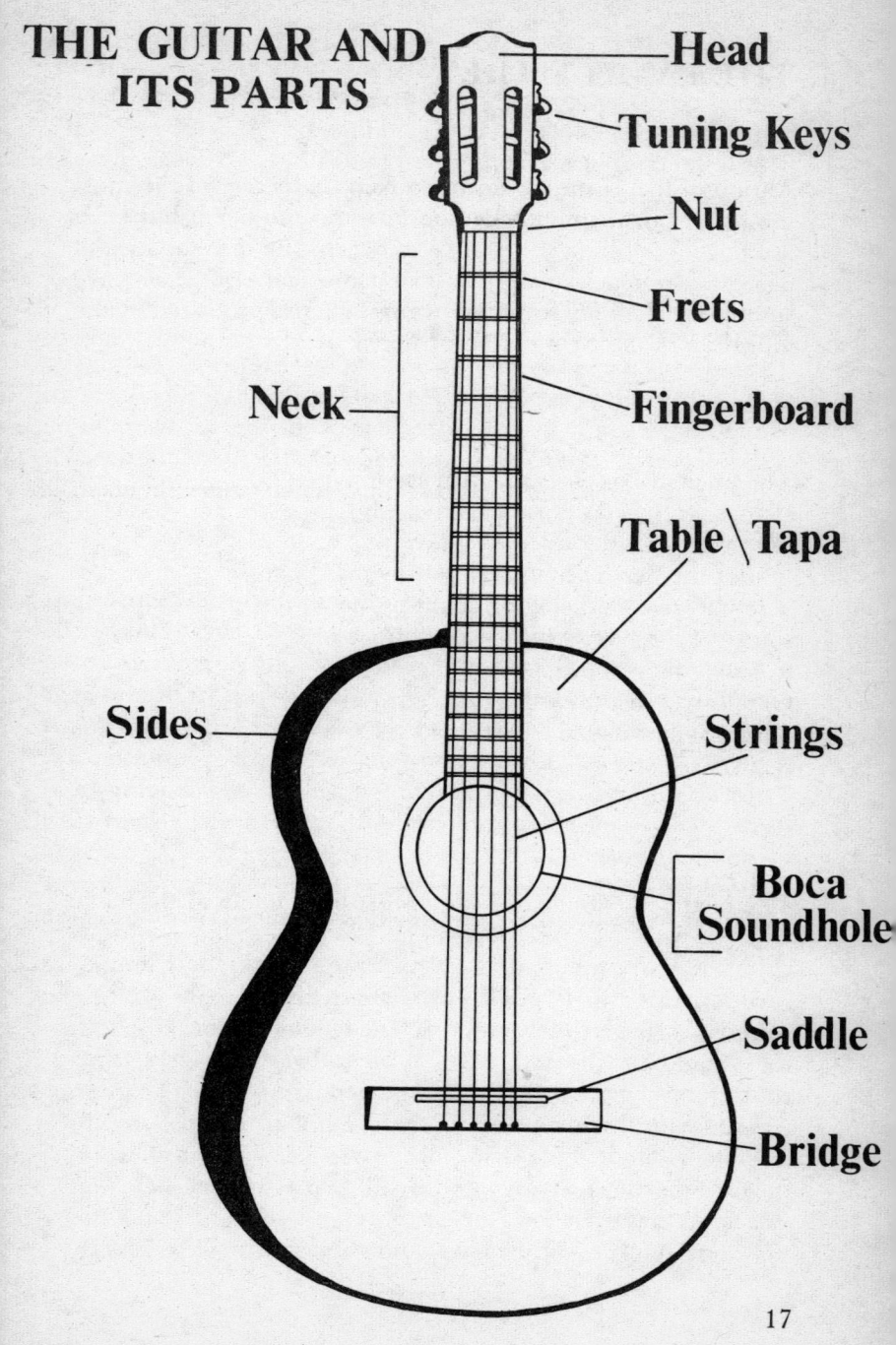

- Head
- Tuning Keys
- Nut
- Frets
- Fingerboard
- Neck
- Table \ Tapa
- Sides
- Strings
- Boca Soundhole
- Saddle
- Bridge

THE FAMILY TREE

Although the guitar could be looked on as one of the most modern of instruments, in one form or another it has been around a very long time. It is quite possible that the idea of using a stretched string to make a musical note may have stemmed originally from the twanging noise produced by the vibration of the string of an ordinary hunting bow.

The ancient **Greek lyre**, with several strings stretched across a box which made the sound louder and gave it more tone, is an obvious step forward. The player would sing or chant to the sound of the lyre, which was thought to have magical properties. The Greeks weren't far wrong there, in my opinion, because music is in a very real sense, magic.

The next most important step must have come at the stage when it was realised that the pitch of a string could be changed, made higher in fact, by shortening its length temporarily. In order to do this a long neck was added to the existing sound box, the strings being stretched along this neck, so that they could be pressed down onto it by the fingers, thus shortening the part which was allowed to vibrate. The main trouble with this method was that, although it succeeded in raising the pitch of the string, there was a deadening effect on the tone produced and it was difficult to play in tune. It was at this point that some long forgotten genius — and I do not use the word lightly — must have come up with the idea of **frets**, bars placed across the neck, which came into contact with the string when it was pressed down and produced a purer, more ringing sound that was also in tune.

You will gain some idea of just how long ago this all must have happened when I tell you that stone carvings have been discovered dating as far back as the Hittite Empire of 1,400 B.C. in which a fretted instrument like a guitar is depicted. That's nearly three and a half thousand years ago!

Thus we have the beginnings of three distinct families of stringed instruments. First the lyre, developing into the different types of **harp**; the long-necked stringed instrument developing into the **violin** family; and the long-necked **fretted** instrument from which the entire family of present-day fretted instruments is descended, including the **lute**, the **banjo**, the **ukelele**, the **mandolin** and the **guitar** in its different forms.

The lute is the fretted instrument you are most likely to see in old books and paintings. It was one of the most popular instruments of the Middle Ages and even today its sweet sound conjures up memories of wandering minstrels and lands of Romantic Legend.

On the face of it a lute looks like a different instrument, with its bowl-like, half-egg shaped body quite unlike the usual waisted shape of the guitar. But there are great similarities in the ways it is played and held. It is interesting to note that the lute was brought to Europe by the Arabs between the eighth and thirteenth centuries, during their occupation of the southern part of Spain which is known as Andalucia. Doubly so, because alongside the more obvious legacy of the Moorish occupation, such as the magnificent palaces of the Alhambra in Granada and the castles in Seville and Almeria, these instruments were obviously forerunners of the guitar. Furthermore, this country of Andalucia was destined to make two major contributions without which the classical Spanish guitar as we know it today would probably never have existed.

Although undoubtedly a beautiful instrument the lute had its disadvantages. From the physical point of view it was extremely fragile and hardly suited to the rough and tumble of a travelling musician's life. The bowl-shaped body was constructed of thin laths of wood held together by strips of vellum and glue and was so light as to be almost of eggshell consistency. It would seldom have less than a dozen strings and could be very temperamental in the matter of tuning for a number of reasons, not the least of which were the poor quality of the strings available and the flimsiness of the instrument's structure. An ancient music book says that if a man owned a lute for 60 years he would spend 40 of them tuning it, adding that a good lute was as expensive to maintain as a horse!

It is not surprising, therefore, that the popularity of the lute began to wane on the arrival of that other family of stringed instruments, the **keyboards**, which whilst they might lack in portability had great advantages in stability of tuning and robustness of sound.

The guitar, on the other hand, with only four strings at that time, and a simpler construction that was also stronger, became the instrument of the common people and was used for strumming dance music and accompanying songs — a direct forerunner of the present day Flamenco style of playing, and of course of today's Folk singer and his inevitable guitar.

Changing musical fashion led to the adoption of the guitar by the court of Louis XIV of France in the late seventeenth century, but it was not until the nineteenth century that the so-called Golden Age of the guitar began, with the virtuoso composers like Aguado, Sor, Carcassi, Carulli and Giuliani, whose music is still performed today in concert halls. Interesting to note that the great violinist Paganini was also a guitarist of some celebrity and said, '*I love it for its harmony; it is the constant companion of my travels.*'

The guitar at that time was rather quiet and lacking in tone because of its small size and this meant that it was only really suitable for playing in the normal sized sitting room. Thus, although the music being written for the instrument would have been good enough to attract large, concert hall-sized audiences, the guitar itself was not yet ready to fulfil that role. But a revolution was at hand, and it is here that our story takes us back again to Andalucia, to the ancient provincial capital of Almeria, a city which even today manages to preserve a certain timeless remoteness from the frantic tide of modernity. In the early 1850's Almeria must have been considered remote indeed, and certainly an unlikely source for a development of such tremendous proportions in the history of the guitar.

Antonio Torres Jurado, known to us as Torres, was born and lived all of his life in Almeria between the years of 1817 and 1892, and in that time he invented the Spanish guitar as we know it today. I say **invented** because the changes in style and shape of the instrument brought about by Torres were far too great to be classed as mere innovations. Torres was not in fact a professional maker of guitars, but a cabinet maker, however he was in the truest sense an **amateur** of the guitar. No-one really knows how or why he came to his conclusions, but Torres decided that the guitar as it was then constructed was all wrong.

It was too small, the upper and lower bouts — the shoulders and hips of the guitar — were very nearly equal in size, and the body was too shallow.

He also had a theory that the **tapa**, the top of the guitar, was the most important part of the instrument from the point of view of sound production. To prove this point he made a guitar shaped box out of *papier mache* which turned out to produce a good tone when he glued one of his fine **tapas** onto it.

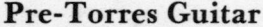

Pre-Torres Guitar

Torres Guitar

The sound of the Torres guitar proved so superior that other guitar makers soon began to adopt his plan, and indeed to this day it is the Torres model, with slight individual differences of dimension which is used by most makers.

So now, with the modern guitar available a second miracle appeared from Andalucia in the person of **Andres Segovia**, who was born in Linares, but lived for most of his boyhood in the beautiful city of Granada, which must have provided him with a great inspiration for the future. It is generally acknowledged that Segovia's life and work have been the central driving force, the fountainhead from which the present day eminence of the classical Spanish guitar has sprung. He has popularised the instrument through his concerts all over the world and his recordings. He has acted as Maestro to the next generation of players like **Julian Bream** and **John Williams** and he has increased the repertoire of the guitar by making transcriptions of classical pieces and also by persuading eminent composers to create works especially for the instrument. All of this work he sums up jestingly by saying that he rescued the guitar from the Gipsies.

I have been speaking until now largely about the classical Spanish guitar, but we must not forget its two American cousins, the **Steel Strung Acoustic** and the **Electric** guitars. These have had an impact on popular music all over the world, and are to be found playing with just about any possible combination of instruments and styles.

The **Steel Strung Acoustic guitar** in its modern form grew up largely from the efforts of a group of European instrument makers who settled in America around the middle of the nineteenth century. It is larger and more heavily built than its Spanish counterpart, and has a more penetrating tone. This means that it is more suited to many popular styles, and you will find today that nearly all Pop, Folk and Country players who use acoustic guitars play a steel strung instrument.

There are many makers of this type of guitar now, but the most commonly used pattern was developed by the descendants of one of those original settlers, **C.F. Martin**. His firm still makes excellent guitars to this day, but it was in the 1930's that they started making the larger Dreadnaught models which compare to the Torres guitar as the standard in their own field. By the way, they became known as the Dreadnaughts because they appeared to be as 'strong as a battleship'.

**Solid Body
Electric Guitars**

The other type of guitar, made and developed in the U.S.A. is the **Electric guitar**, which has exploded into popularity in the last thirty years in a way that has changed the whole sound and appearance of Pop music. With an Electric guitar and the aid of an amplifier the guitarist can make as loud a sound as he or his audience want.

He can also move around the stage more, which means that a player like Chuck Berry is able to entertain his fans as much with his antics on stage as with his guitar playing.

Because it no longer has a soundbox to make the sounds of its strings louder the solid Electric guitar may seem to have little in common with other guitars, but it is still basically the same instrument. Many of the most popular models still look very much like our traditional idea of a guitar. The neck is the same, and although the bodies can be almost any shape, they still have the curves which you can recognise as belonging to a guitar.

There are growing musical links between one kind of guitar and another. The virtuoso classical guitarist John Williams has recently taken to using an Electric guitar with his group SKY, which plays a mixture of classical and Rock music. Also you will find that many humbler players like myself and Nick may move as the mood takes us from the classical guitar to the steel strung acoustic, and particularly for myself, to my beloved hollow-body Chet Atkins Model Gretsch Electric.

Each type of guitar has its virtues and its place in the great overall plan of music.

WHICH GUITAR FOR YOU?

We spoke briefly in the previous chapters about the different types of guitar, and of the fact that each kind of guitar is particularly designed to be suitable for a certain type of music. Bearing this in mind, your choice of a guitar will be governed to a large extent by the kind of music which interests you personally. For **interests** we should perhaps substitute *gives you pleasure* because obviously you are going to enjoy your own playing much more if you are making the kind of musical sounds you like to hear.

THE SPANISH GUITAR

The first type of guitar we deal with must naturally be the Spanish guitar — the instrument of Torres and Segovia.

This is a nylon strung guitar with a warm, sensitive tone, used for playing in the Classical solo manner as by Segovia, Julian Bream, John Williams, etc., in Flamenco playing, as by Paco de Lucia, Paco Pena, etc., or as an accompanying instrument by some Folk singers like Paul Simon.

Spanish Concert Guitar

Comparing these three different uses you will realise that the Spanish guitar is a versatile instrument and that the sound it produces can be modified to a great extent by the demands and technique of the person who is playing it. Compare the gentle, but pleasant strummings of the average Folk singer with the grandeur of the sound of Segovia playing the Bach Chaconne, and then think again of the fiery rhythms of Flamenco as played by such artists as Paco Pena and you will appreciate that the Spanish guitar possesses at least three distinct personalities.

The strings of a Spanish guitar are made of nylon, the first three of **single filament nylon**, like fishing line, of different thicknesses and the bottom three of **nylon floss wound with silver or bronze** to give them the extra density needed to produce the lower sound. Nylon strings are played by the right hand thumb and fingers.

> A plectrum should not be used on a Spanish guitar — neither should a Spanish guitar **ever be strung with steel strings**. The instrument is lightly built to take the lesser tension of nylon strings and it could suffer permanent damage under the stress of steel strings.

Many beginners find that nylon strings are easier on the fingers, causing less of the soreness we talked about earlier, but whether or not you choose a Spanish guitar to begin on really does depend on the nature of your musical ambitions. If you are keen on Classical, Flamenco or Folk song accompaniment, a nylon strung guitar should suit you fine, but if you are definitely headed in the direction of Rock, Pop or Jazz you would be best to start off from the beginning with a steel strung instrument.

THE STEEL STRUNG ACOUSTIC GUITAR

The first and probably most suitable instrument of the steel strung type is the **Round Hole Acoustic guitar**, sometimes known as the 'Jumbo' or 'Dreadnaught'.

These are very similar in appearance to the traditional Spanish guitar, but more heavily built to withstand the extra tension of steel strings and often with a larger body. Another important point is that the fingerboard of a steel strung guitar should be narrower and slightly curved, a fact which makes it easier to play in some respects than a Spanish guitar, particularly when dealing with moving chord passages.

Basically, as I mentioned earlier, the steel strung acoustic is a U.S. development and it has become the traditional instrument for the playing of Blues, Ragtime and Country styles. This is the instrument that I first found so attractive in the hands of the Singing Cowboys, Roy Rogers and Gene Autry. You may never have even heard of them, but someone who has followed on in their tradition is **Glen Campbell**, a terrific guitar player and good singer.

A steel strung acoustic can be played either with the fingers of the right hand or with a **pick** or **plectrum**.

A plectrum is a piece of plastic or shell which is held between the fingers and thumb of the right hand. It can be very useful in the playing of single note solos or rhythmic chords and it does tend to produce a louder, brighter sound than the unaided fingers.

A pick is usually made of plastic and fits onto the thumb like a ring. Its main use is to give extra volume to the three bass strings when playing song accompaniments. I have experimented with it for solo playing, but I find it much more clumsy for this than the unaided thumb.

Like the Spanish guitar the Acoustic guitar is completely self-contained. It can be taken anywhere and played anywhere. There's nothing to compare with the sound of a guitar in the open air, by the way — so take it out with you on fine days. I **always** do. On the other hand, the next two types of guitar depend to a large extent upon the assistance of an **amplifier** to produce a reasonable sound. From the beginners point of view this implies an extra and not entirely necessary expense.

You can learn all of the basics on a steel strung guitar in any of the styles mentioned above, and by that time you will certainly have some better idea of the direction in which you want to go musically. At that point you may decide to stay with the acoustic instrument, or go in for amplification. Even here you have a choice, because you could keep your original instrument and have it fitted with a pickup which will enable you to play through an amplifier, or you can trade in your acoustic for a semi-acoustic or a solid guitar.

THE SEMI-ACOUSTIC GUITAR

The **Semi-Acoustic** is mostly favoured by Jazz players. It has a very slim body which will generally give only sufficient un-amplified sound for practice purposes. It has steel strings, and it is the magnetic vibrations of these conveyed to the amplifier by the **pickup** (or pickups) which produces the main sound.

Normally played with a plectrum it is used for both rhythm and single note solo playing in Jazz groups, although there is a growing trend amongst Jazz soloists, inspired no doubt by the work of **Joe Pass**, to play the Semi-Acoustic electric guitar with the fingers of the right hand, a style which increases the self-contained qualities of the instrument and makes it into what has been described as a **Lap Piano**.

THE SOLID ELECTRIC GUITAR

The guitar that most young people will automatically think of when the word is mentioned is the Solid Electric, which is seen in a vast variety of forms in today's Rock and Pop groups.

The Solid depends entirely on an amplifier for its sound. For this reason a beginner buying a Solid must be prepared at the same time to go to the expense of buying an amplifier, which may cost him as much, or even more than the guitar itself. This being so, I would not happily recommend any complete beginner to start off with a Solid guitar.

Since the sound of a Solid guitar is not governed in any way by the shape of the body there are any number of variations in its appearance.

So there you have the four basic types of guitar, and you will have gathered from my remarks about them that your choice as a beginner is really between the first two — either a nylon strung Spanish, or a Steel Strung Acoustic. Although that may seem to have narrowed down the choice considerably, you will find in practice that when you go out seriously looking for the guitar you are going to buy, you will be met with a bewildering variety of instruments. Ideally, if you have a teacher, or a friend who plays in the kind of style you're aiming at, you would be well advised to get one of them to go along with you on your guitar hunting expedition. They will be able to try out the guitars whilst you listen to them, and also to give their opinion on playability in matters such as **action** and **tonal response**.

Failing such help, do at least make sure that you go to a shop where they know and care about guitars, rather than one that is mainly devoted to the selling of records and tapes and keeps a few instruments on the side. It is difficult to be precise about price. If you are buying from the kind of dealer I suggest, you should get good value for money and obtain as good a guitar as possible for what you have to spend. Here again your friend or teacher will be able to help you with advice on prices.

> You may not necessarily want to buy a new guitar, and you would be quite right in thinking that you could save a considerable amount of money by buying a **second hand one**. Only one of my four guitars is a new one, and that was built especially for me. On the other hand, you could **also waste quite a bit of money** by buying something that is faulty or quite unsuitable. Here again, enlist the help of someone who knows about guitars and take his advice **before** buying.

It would also be nice to have a good **case** for your instrument, and this may cost you several pounds more. BUT if you approach the guitar in the way I recommend the case will only be used when you are transporting the guitar from one place to another. This should be the purpose of a case, NOT storage, except in tropical conditions, where it may need protection from extremes of heat and humidity. A guitar put away in a case is a guitar forgotten and not used, and therefore not practised upon. If the guitar is to become part of your life it must become part of your furniture, readily available to be picked up at any time during the day. This is not to say that you should not be careful with your instrument. It must not be propped up somewhere so that it can be knocked over, jumped on by the cat, sat on by Dad, cooked by a radiator, or used as a cricket bat by little Johnny.

TUNING UP

There is a sign in the window of our local music shop which reads: *GUITAR TUNING SERVICE*. I mention that because apart from anything else this chapter alone is going to save you the price of the entire book several times over.

I know this doesn't apply to you, but it comes as something of a shock to a lot of people when they realise that the fact that they have paid thirty, forty, or fifty pounds for a brand new guitar does not in any way guarantee that it will be in tune when they get it home. No really, I'm not joking. I wish I had a pound for every time I've heard a beginner say in genuine surprise and puzzlement: 'But I thought it was in tune when I bought it!'

It probably was, but any number of things can have happened to change that tuning in the process of taking the guitar to your home. It's the easiest thing in the world to catch one of the tuning pegs when you're putting an instrument in its case, for instance. And, however careful you are, there's no doubt that changes in temperature affect tuning. Merely taking it out of the warm shop into the cooler open air could have caused a change. For these and other fairly obvious reasons it is a nonsense to take a guitar to a shop to have it tuned. Now that you have your own instrument the first thing you should learn is how to tune it for yourself. You may find this task difficult at first — **most people do** — but as with everything else connected with the guitar you will improve with practice.

Put at its simplest, the **pitch** of the sound that a string makes is controlled by how **tight** it is. A slack string makes a low sound, which becomes higher and higher as it is tightened.

You can produce the same sort of effect by hooking a rubber band over your two thumbs and plucking it with a finger, at the same time moving your thumbs apart to stretch the band. As you do so you cannot help but notice that the sound of its twanging becomes higher and higher. Eventually it will break if you keep on stretching it.

Here again, the same thing applies to a guitar string. Something which you don't want to happen too often, because it will cost you rather more to replace than a rubber band. Bearing this in mind it is important to turn the tuning pegs gently, and to make quite certain by the methods outlined below that you are turning the peg **in the right direction**. Otherwise you could go on tightening the string until it eventually goes bang!

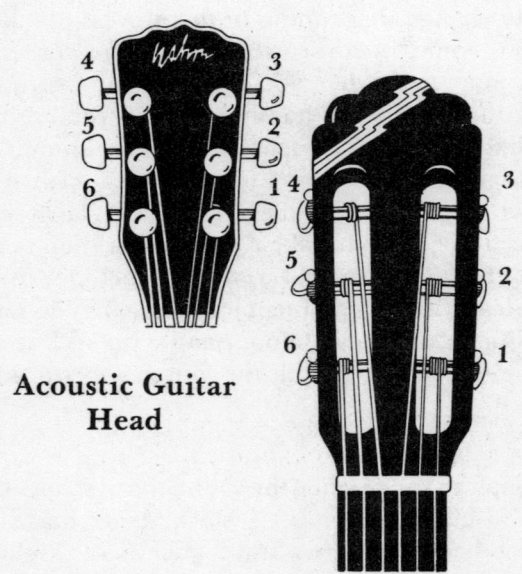

Acoustic Guitar Head

Spanish Guitar Head

The six strings of your guitar are tuned individually by the **tuning pegs**. In the old days these were literally pegs, fitted directly into the wood of the head, and they were liable to slip, making tuning even more difficult.

Matters are made easier for us today by the **machine heads**, those little geared mechanisms you will see at the head of your guitar. These differ slightly in shape between an Acoustic guitar and a Spanish, but they are basically the same thing.

Some Flamenco guitars use the old type of peg head even today, but I can see no practical reason for this and I have an idea that it is really an affectation intended to give an air of the 'Primitive'.

The tuning pegs should correspond to the strings as shown in the diagrams.

NEVER put a string onto the wrong peg, because if you do you won't know which string you are tightening.

And **NEVER** insert a string into the hole of the peg so that it winds on in the wrong direction.

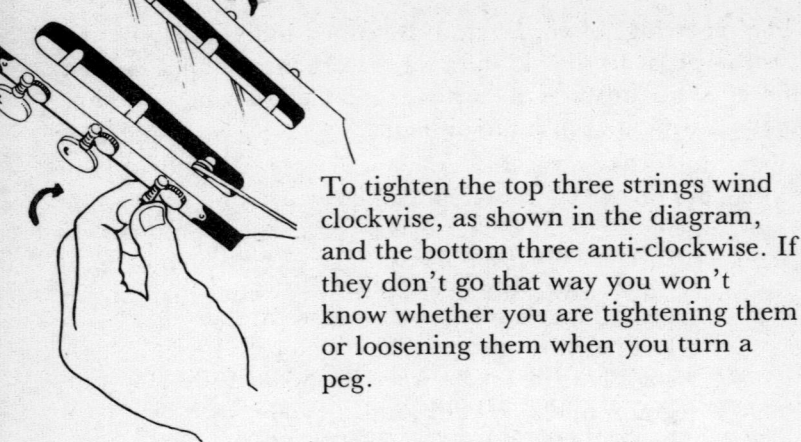

To tighten the top three strings wind clockwise, as shown in the diagram, and the bottom three anti-clockwise. If they don't go that way you won't know whether you are tightening them or loosening them when you turn a peg.

If the above seems quite obvious to you, you're clearly a lot smarter than I am, because at one time or another I've made **all** of the mistakes mentioned above!

The guitar is a bass instrument, but for the sake of convenience the music for it is written in the treble clef. This means that the notes actually sound an octave lower than they are written. The strings of the guitar are tuned as shown below:

It is important to understand the numbering of the strings, and to appreciate fully that the **1st string is the thinnest**, the one with the highest sound, and the **6th the thickest**, the one with the lowest sound. Thus, although both the 1st and 6th strings are tuned to the note E, they are in fact two octaves apart.

TUNING WITH A KEYBOARD

I cannot pretend to you that you will find this process easy at first, unless your ear is already well trained in identifying pitch, but do persevere. First make up your mind whether the note of your string is higher or lower than that produced by the keyboard. Ideally it should be lower, because it is better to approach the correct tuning from below, rather than above.

So, begin with your 1st, E string and compare its sound with that of the E on the keyboard. Is it higher or lower? If you're not certain you might try playing other notes on the keyboard until you find one that corresponds. If that is higher, slacken the string off until it sounds **below** the keyboard note. Then, tighten it gradually until it matches. By coming up to the pitch in this way rather than tuning downwards the guitar string is more likely to retain its correct note after tuning.

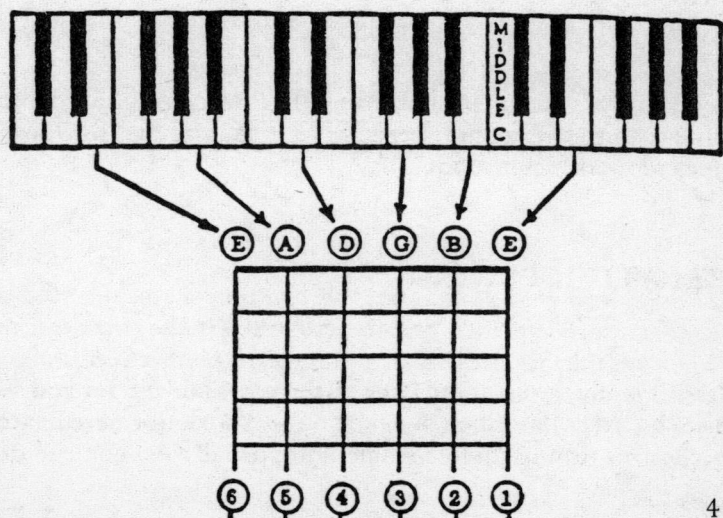

Happy about your top E? Right, then let's move onto the second, B string.

> First the note on the keyboard, then play the note of the 2nd string on the guitar. Is it high, or low? If it's low, tighten it gradually until the two sounds match up. Sometimes, when you get quite close but not precisely on pitch and the two notes are sounded at once you will detect a kind of harshness in the combined sound, whereas once they are together, in what we call unison, the sound is sweet and pure. Difficult at first to define these different states, but your ear will soon become able to identify them immediately. If the string is high in pitch — too near to that of the E you have already tuned, then slacken it off and bring it up again gradually until the sounds match.

Next move down to the 3rd, G string, and carry out the same routine; then the 4th, the D, the 5th, the A, and the 6th, the final E. When you have tuned this last one you can match it up with the 1st, string E. As I mentioned above, they should be the same note, but two octaves apart.

By the way, you will probably find the lower strings harder to tune than the high ones, because your ear will find the lower ones more difficult to identify.

RELATIVE TUNING

It isn't really necessary to have all the notes laid out for you on a keyboard as described above. You will no doubt have heard orchestras tuning up to a single note, usually A. You can do something similar. Starting from one note, preferably the G, B or E of your top three strings you can use the method of Relative Tuning, which is without a doubt the most accurate way of tuning a guitar.

Relative Tuning ensures that a guitar is in tune with itself, a most important and desirable situation, because if it isn't in tune with itself nothing you play on it will sound right. In single note playing an out of tune string should be immediately apparent to the ear when a passage across the strings is played. And when playing chords, an out of tune string will make the chord sound wrong, destroying its harmony. Two out of tune strings will give a total effect of something like musical toothache.

Relative Tuning works through a method of matching the sounds of adjacent strings, as shown diagrammatically below:

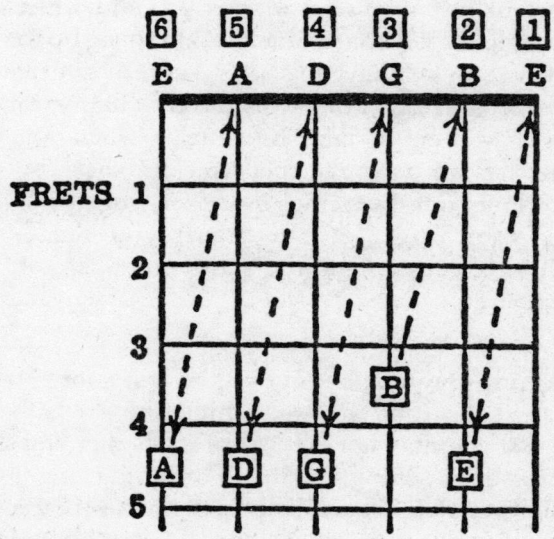

With this method, if any one of your strings is in tune, the others can be tuned from it. The best string to start from is the 3rd, or G, although any of the others will serve the purpose if necessary. It really depends what note is available to you, in either a **tuning fork** or a **pitch pipe**. Or of course, once again from a keyboard, in which case you will use just a single note to tune the one string, and then tune the others from it.

Starting from the G string has always seemed the most convenient way of tuning to me. I then work upwards through the B and E strings before coming back to the lower ones and working downwards. So, tune the G string to your satisfaction and then press the first finger of your left hand down on that string just behind the 4th fret and pluck the string. This will give you the note B, which is the correct pitch for the 2nd or B string.

Now, in just the same way as you did when tuning to the keyboard tune the 2nd string up to that B. You will have to sound it several times, of course. It really doesn't matter how many, so long as you get it right. Eventually, when you have the two notes matched you can check by sounding both the strings in unison (together), with **your finger on the 4th fret of the G string, of course**, and the 2nd string open, or unfingered.

The main thing to remember in this process is not to try and rush things. Take your time and think about what you're doing. At first you may not even be sure whether you should be tightening or loosening a string in order to bring it to the pitch of the given note (in this case the B on the 4th fret of the 3rd string). If you are uncertain, **don't** go on tightening the string until it pops. Better to slacken it off and approach the correct note again from below, as I suggested above. The unison between the two strings when they are correctly tuned will soon become easy to recognise. That is just a matter of your ear becoming used to this kind of work.

> When you are satisfied with the tuning of the 2nd string, place your finger down close behind the 5th fret on that same string. This will raise its pitch to E, which is the note you need to tune the 1st string. Carry out this process in the same way as described above. Be gentle with the tuning peg, turning it a little at a time . . .

After the E string has been tuned your top three strings should all be in tune. I say **should** because this may not necessarily be so, especially if the strings on your guitar are new, in which case they may have stretched. And there are other little hazards like a machine head slipping slightly, or even, (dare I say it?) adjusted in error. When you're really used to the guitar a quick strum across the top three strings with your thumb will immediately tell you if anything like this has happened, but at this stage the best thing to do is to give them another quick check by testing the unisons — 4th fret, 3rd string and 5th fret, 2nd string.

Now it is time to turn your attention to the bass, lower side of the guitar.

> When correctly tuned, the note at the 5th fret of the 4th string should correspond with the open 3rd string. If they don't sound in unison adjust the 4th string upwards or downwards until they do. **Remember that this time it is the lower string that you should be adjusting, rather than the 3rd which you have already tuned.**

That may seem obvious to you, but such mistakes can and do happen.

When the 4th string is in tune, finger the 5th at the 5th fret and match it with the open 4th in the same way. Then the 6th string, which is fingered likewise on the 5th fret.

At this point you might take another look at the main Relative Tuning Diagram on page 43. It is useful to remember that, as shown there, with **sole exception of the 3rd string**, which is **fingered on the 4th fret**, the equivalent or unison note is obtained in each case by fingering the lower string at the 5th fret.

PITCH PIPES

Most music shops will be able to sell you a set of six small pipes which are tuned to the notes of the six open strings, and on the face of it this appears to be a simple, uncomplicated method of tuning. However, you will find that in practice this is not really the case, because the sound of the pitch pipes, although it may be correct in pitch, is so different in quality as to be difficult to identify with the sound of a plucked guitar string. If you do use pitch pipes, because there is nothing else available, then I would suggest that you use them to tune **one only** of your strings, preferably the G, and then tune the rest by Relative Tuning as described above.

TUNING FORKS

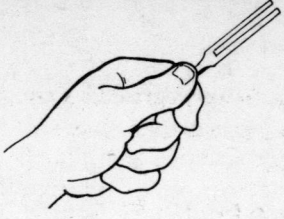

Tuning forks are the time-honoured method of tuning, of course, but if you are going to use one I suggest that you ask someone who knows, your music teacher, for instance, to show you the correct method.

Another slight difficulty lies in getting hold of a tuning fork which is pitched to one of your open strings. I have one, for instance, which is pitched at the note C. This means that if I want to tune the guitar from it, I have to begin by tuning the note on the first fret of the 2nd string.

Now that may be all right for me, but it is not the sort of complication in which I would willingly involve you at your stage of development. If you can find a tuning fork pitched to the G of your 3rd string, all well and good, you can then proceed as outlined in the Relative Tuning instruments — otherwise, use another method.

ON TUNING IN GENERAL

It may seem to you that this explanation of the process of tuning is rather long-winded, but I can assure you that if you are to make music on your guitar it is an operation of prime importance. **You should never take tuning for granted**. Strings can slip at the machine heads, they can stretch or contract in sympathy with atmospheric conditions, as indeed can the guitar itself. And any of these factors will affect tuning.

Always take time to check your tuning before beginning to play. Just how much time will depend on your musical ear and your experience as a player. At first you will have to go through the complete Relative Tuning routine, but as you progress the playing of any six string chord will tell you immediately whether or not your guitar is in tune. During a playing session an experienced player is constantly checking his tuning and adjusting it as necessary. He is able to do this because his trained ear is able to detect a faulty string tuning immediately.

ELECTRONIC TUNERS

If you want to get through this entire operation quite painlessly and are prepared to spend £20 upwards to do so, there are a number of Electronic Tuners on the market. With one of these all you have to do is tune your strings one by one until they centre up the meter needle on the gadget's dial **and they will automatically be in tune**.

These instruments are particularly useful for anyone who plays in a group, when there may be a lot of noise going on and several people are trying to tune in at the same time, so that you may not even be able to hear the note you are playing. But the Tuner *can*, and that needle will centre up if you're in tune. On the other hand, the lone guitarist, unless he is a complete tin ear, shouldn't really need such a scientific marvel to get him in reasonable tune.

BEGINNING TO PLAY

You may think from what you see on TV and in magazine pictures that it is possible to play the guitar in practically any kind of position, including standing on your head.

Possible, yes, but not really desirable. After all there's no point in making things unnecessarily hard for yourself at the beginning, is there? The best thing you can do is to start off by using one of two seated positions.

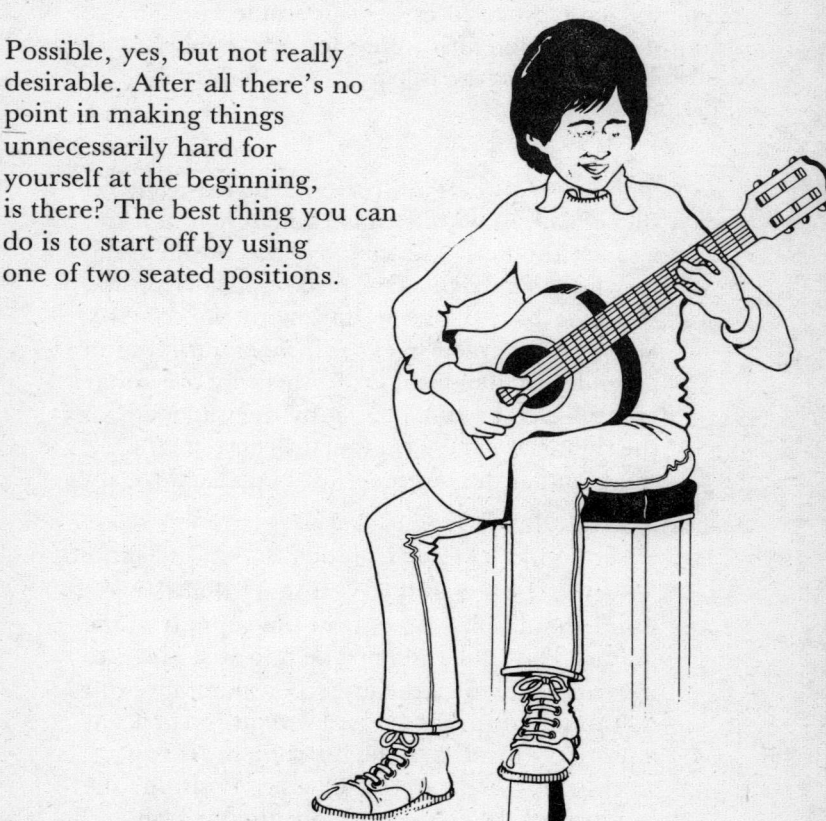

The first of these is the Classic position which has become accepted by Classical Spanish guitar players after many years of experience as the most comfortable and efficient way of playing.

The stool shown in the illustration is really optional. I used to use one all the time, but I must admit that of late years I tend to be more interested in getting a chair of the correct height so that I can rest my left foot on the floor. Most footstools are made in a collapsible form, but they are so much extra baggage to carry nevertheless.

The waist of the guitar should sit naturally on the left thigh, with the instrument held upright against the body, so that you are not bending forward. The right arm rests naturally on the broadest part of the guitar, with the forearm able to swing freely over the front of the guitar in a pendulum like fashion. In this way the guitar is supported at four points: by the underside of the right arm, at the front of the chest, on the left thigh and at the bottom of its body by the right thigh.

It cannot be stressed too strongly that the **left hand** should play no part in the support of the guitar. The left hand must be free at all times to move up and down the fingerboard, and it can't do this job properly if it is also required to act as a prop for the neck of the instrument. If you are sitting in the correct Classic position the removal of the left hand from the neck should have no effect at all on the support of the instrument. You might like to experiment with this.

The second, and most popular seated position, used by the great majority of players of the steel strung guitar in the Folk, Blues and Jazz fields is shown below.

In this instance you simply sit in a chair of suitable height — that is, one which will allow your foot to rest flat on the floor — cross your right leg over your left, and rest the waist of the guitar on your right thigh. Your right arm rests on the broadest part of the guitar, as in the Classic position, helping to hold the instrument firmly against your chest.

Once again, your left arm should play no part in the support of the guitar, but should be free to move. It is also a good idea to keep the left elbow tucked in towards the body, because this tends to bring the left hand into a good fingering position in relation to the neck of the guitar.

Yes, I know that the groups stand up with their axes on slings and hanging down to their knees, but I never yet saw Segovia, Julian Bream, Barney Kessel, or any of the great Flamenco players perform in a standing position. Later on, when you're really familiar with the guitar and so good that you can afford to sacrifice a certain amount of your technique, you can play in whatever position you prefer — even standing on your head, if you feel so inclined.

THE RIGHT HAND

To begin with, the right hand
should be allowed to hang
relaxed over the soundhole,
with the fingers at right angles
to the strings.

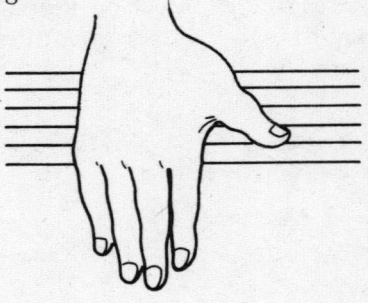

From this position the fingers
should be slightly adjusted
until they take up the position
shown below, with the thumb
well forward, the first finger
on the 3rd string, the second
on the 2nd string and the third
on the 1st string as shown.

In this way the thumb plays the three bottom strings and each of the three fingers has its own string right next to it, ready to be struck with the minimum of movement. The strings are literally under the fingers, as shown in the guitarist's eye view:

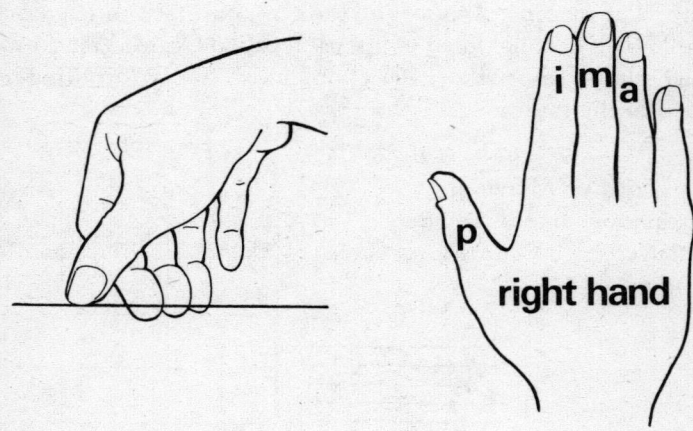

From this position, with the thumb and fingers resting on the correct strings make a downward stroke with your thumb on the 6th string, the one on top as you are looking down at it — the thickest one. Then pluck the first three strings with your three fingers — this time with an upward movement. By allowing the sound of these four strings to ring out you will have made your first chord on the guitar.

A chord is made up of three or more notes, and as in this case, each of the strings provides a single note. Chords are used in song accompaniments to provide a rhythmic and harmonic background to the melody, whether it is sung or played on another musical instrument. Chords are quite easy to play on the guitar, and you will learn many of them in the course of this book.

CHORD WINDOWS

The chord you have just played is called E Minor, and in guitar music it is written **Em**. You will learn more about these names later, but at the moment it is sufficient to say that the names of chords are related to the names of the notes within them. The playing of chords on the guitar is made much more simple by a graphic form of notation called Chord Windows, which shows you what each chord looks like on the fingerboard of the guitar.

The chord you have just played looks like this, when portrayed by a Chord Window:

E minor

It is pretty obvious, even at first glance, that Chord Windows are based on a pictorial representation of the guitar fingerboard. Reading from left to right the vertical lines indicate the strings 6th, 5th, 4th, and so on. The top horizontal line is a double one to indicate that it represents the **Nut** — that is the piece of plastic or bone which divides the vibrating section of the string from the part which goes on to the tuning head. The other horizontal lines represent the frets, which are numbered 1st, 2nd, 3rd, and so on.

54

You will have noticed two X's directly above the 5th and 4th strings in the diagram. These are to indicate that in this particular chord those strings are not sounded. In contrast, over the 6th, 3rd, 2nd, and 1st strings you will see O's. These are to indicate that those four strings are sounded **Open**, or unfingered.

THE LEFT HAND

The first thing to say about the left hand is that the fingernails should be trimmed down close, so that they do not interfere in any way with your left hand fingering. If they are too long they may catch in the strings and cause all sorts of undesirable rattles and buzzes.

The natural position of the left hand is found by bringing the hand up, with the palm facing away from you, until the thumb is in the middle of the back of the neck of the instrument and roughly at right angles to it.

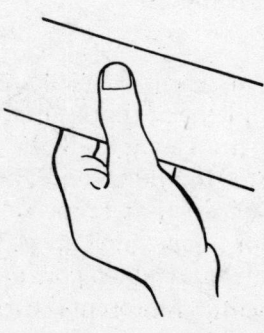

The fingers are then arched around
the neck until they make contact with
the strings, once again at a right
angle, with the first joint of each finger
slightly bent. In this way the pressures
between thumb and fingers balance
each other.

This is the correct Left hand position as used by Classical
guitarists.

If your guitar is a steel strung
model with a thinner neck the
position can be varied slightly
for the sake of comfort, BUT
beware of falling into the
position shown below.

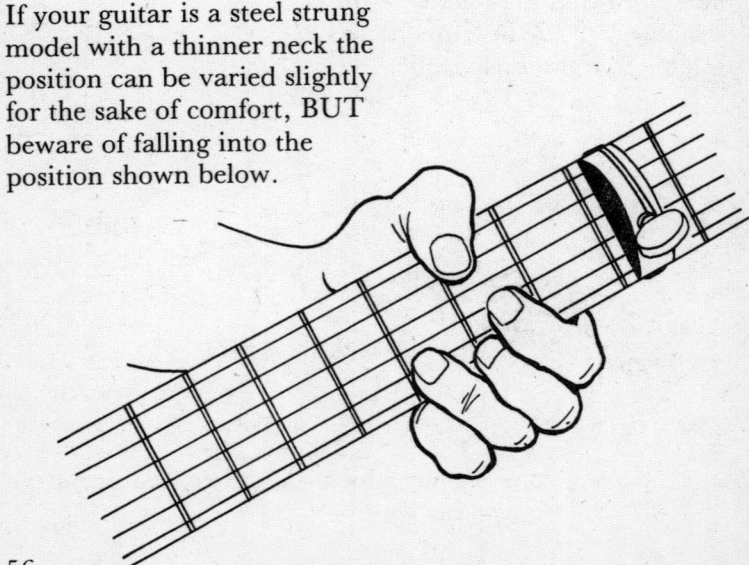

You will see some Jazz players using a position which looks very like this, but they have a good reason **and a great deal more experience**, so that while using the thumb for bass notes on the 6th string they are still able to move around the fingerboard with facility. The great Jazz guitarist Barney Kessel is a case in point, being possessed of a left hand thumb which appears to work quite independently of his fingers and performs the most incredible contortions. In your case, if you start out with the thumb hooked over the fingerboard and the neck of the guitar cradled in the palm of your hand you are starting out with a very bad habit which is sure to restrict the free movement of your left hand. **Only the fleshy part of the thumb contacts the back of the neck, as shown in the diagram**.

Now let us take our first Chord Window and adapt it slightly, like this:

This chord is known as G, or G Major.

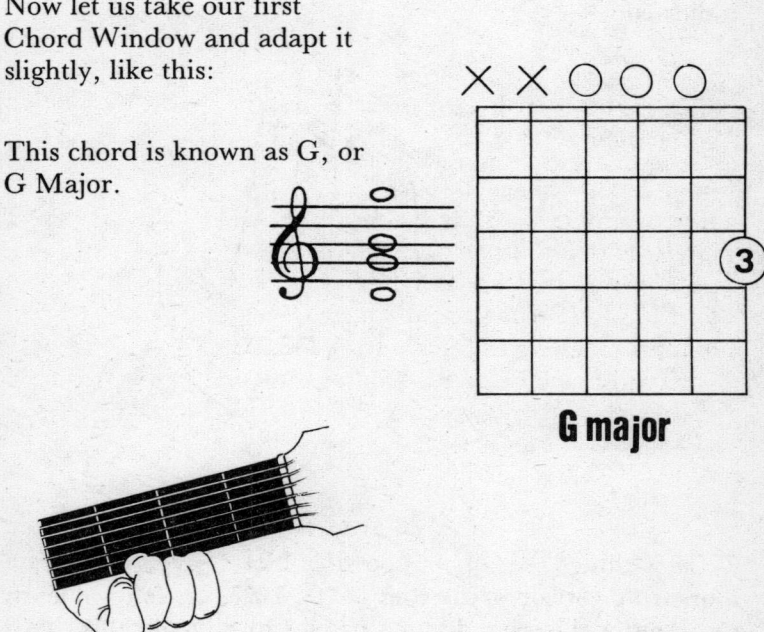

G major

This is what it looks like when you finger it on your guitar.

It is very similar to the open string
chord shown previously, except that in
this case the open 4th string, rather
than the 6th string is sounded by the
thumb, and the 1st string is fingered
at the third fret, as indicated by the
circle in that position in the diagram.
The number inside that circle
indicates that the 3rd finger of the Left
hand should be used for this
purpose — **and no other**.

It is important at this stage
that you should use precisely
the left hand fingering
indicated.

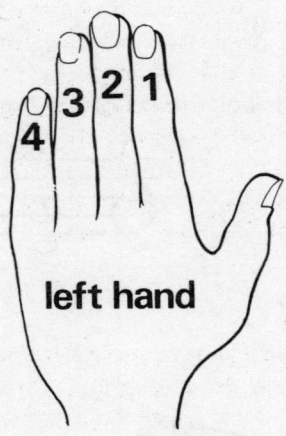

left hand

To keep things as simple as possible I have given you only a
four string version of the chord of G. Later on you will learn
the additional left hand fingering which will make this chord
into a six string one, and that process would be made unnecessarily difficult if you got into the habit of using the wrong
fingers now.

When fingering a string it should be pressed down just **behind, not on**, the fret. This brings the string firmly into contact with the metal of the fret, thus shortening the length of the part of the string that vibrates and making its pitch higher than that of the open string. If you turn to the Fingerboard Diagram on page 61 you will be able to see that by stopping the 1st string at the third fret it produces the note G.

Now, using your thumb alone this time in the right hand, draw it down firmly across the four strings indicated. Remember that in this Chord window the 6th and 5th strings have X's above them, **so they are not sounded**. You should not find any difficulty in producing a musical tone from the 4th, 3rd, and 2nd strings in this chord, but you may find that the 1st gives you nothing more than an inelegant 'phut' sound. If this happens you are probably not pressing down on the string in the right place, or with sufficient firmness. Alternatively it could be that the 2nd string doesn't sound properly. If so, your finger is probably making accidental contact with it and deadening its sound.

We all produce our quota of dead notes, of rattles and buzzes in the beginning, and even later on when we misplace the fingers of our left hand. It is therefore important to learn by your mistakes — to examine in particular just what your left hand was doing wrong when it produced the bad sound **and to correct it there and then**. At all times your goal should be to produce a good sound from the guitar. Once your notes are strong and clear, with good sustaining power, you will know that your left hand fingers are getting it right.

Just how much pressure should your left hand fingers exert on a string? In theory this should be just sufficient to hold the string firmly against the fret and allow it to vibrate freely without buzzes and rattles. In practice of course, your fingers will become sore and there will be times when you find it slightly painful to exert the required pressure. Uncomfortable, but this stage will pass as your finger ends become harder.

Now practise your G chord a few times, before turning on to the next chapter where we shall really be moving on our way, using that chord to play a simple song accompaniment.

**Where To
Find the Notes
on Your
Fingerboard**

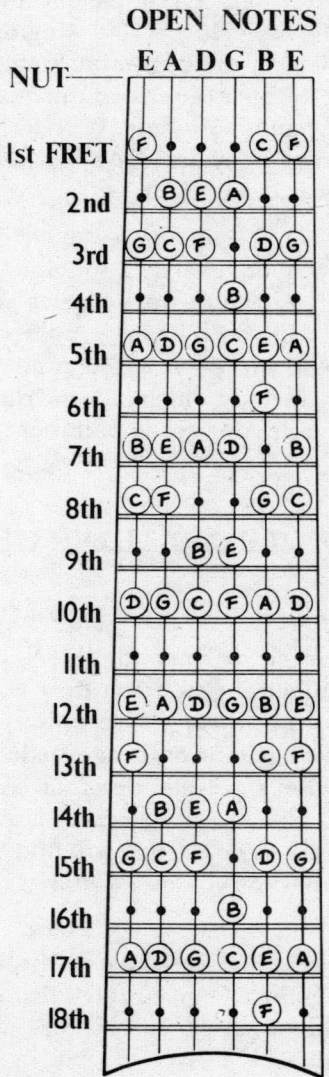

61

SONGS IN G

You should now be ready to try your first song. As I said in the previous chapter, this is a simple one and you probably know its melody already. How's your singing voice, by the way? It's a great help in the beginning stages of guitar playing if you **can** sing, because the easiest things to play on a guitar are simple song accompaniments. With a reasonable voice and a small repertoire of chords you'll soon be able to make a satisfying musical sound.

If like me you're not exactly a songbird, but more of a crow, you're going to have to work harder at your guitar playing because that's all you'll have — unless you're lucky enough to know a friend who plays a Recorder. In that case, he or she could play the melody which I have written in normal musical notation beneath your accompaniment.

A NOTE ON THE READING OF MUSIC

It is not necessary for you to be able to read music yourself at this point, **indeed if you don't ever wish to go any further than the playing of song accompaniments you should be able to get by without reading music indefinitely**. On the other hand, don't get the idea that reading music is a bad thing. If you can already read, or are prepared to put the effort in to learn to do so, you will find that it opens up many new possibilities for you as a guitarist.

If you can't read music at this point, don't worry about it for the time being. Concentrate for now on getting to know the guitar, then later on you can use this knowledge to help you learn music.

TEN IN THE BED

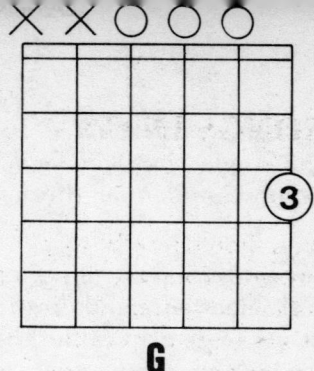

G

HOLD G CHORD

THERE WERE TEN IN THE BED AND THE LITT-LE ONE SAID 'ROLL

OV-ER , ROLL OV-ER !' SO THEY ALL ROLLED OV-ER AND

ONE FELL OUT, THERE WERE . . .

. . . Nine in the bed
And the little one said
'Roll over, roll over!'
So they all rolled over
And one fell out,
    There were

       Eight in the bed . . .
       Seven in the bed . . .
       Six . . . Five . . . Four . . .
       Three . . . Two . . . One . .
       Until 'none'.

As I said earlier, *TEN IN BED* is a very simple tune, so that the single chord of G is enough to provide a reasonable accompaniment all through the song.

What you have to do is to hold your 3rd finger left hand down on that 1st string to give a G chord like the one we have practised, while strumming downwards across the top four strings with your right hand thumb as you sing.

If you perform this strum just anyhow it would sound messy. Tunes have what is called a 'rhythm', which means that they are played or sung at a set speed, with regular beats like a clock ticking, or a heartbeat.

Along with melody and harmony, **rhythm** is one of the essential components that go to make up music. At the present stage of your development what you are learning to do on the guitar is to produce a rhythmic/harmonic background to a song, whilst the melody is provided either by your own voice or your patient friend with his or her Recorder.

What you **are not trying to do here** is to play the tune or melody. Therefore you must follow the beat rather than the tune. In *TEN IN THE BED* the beats come where the diagonal lines / indicate.

If you compare these with the
bar lines in the music you will
see that there are **two** of these
beats to a bar.

This means that rather than following
the individual stresses of the words
you should strum across the chord of
G with your Thumb each time you see
the sign/.

So, to begin playing this song you must first find the beginning note D on your open 4th string and sing or play the
words *There were* . . . Your first strum comes on the word *Ten*,
the second on the word *Bed*, the next on the word *Little* and so
on . . . To show the effect in words:

there were TEN in the BED and the LITTLE one SAID. . . .
        /   /   /   /

The beats come on the words that are shown in capital letters,
to put it another way. Thus you should be producing a
regular rhythm or beat, whilst the words and melody of the
song fit around this beat to form a coherent whole.

TEN IN THE BED is really a singing game, and you will see that at the end of each verse one falls out of the bed, leaving nine, then eight, and so on, until none are left and the song ends. This should give you a lot of good practice in playing your guitar accompaniment and quite a bit of fun at the same time.

Now using the same G chord, but a different rhythm, let's try another song, *LONDON'S BURNING*.

LONDON'S BURNING

If you examine *LONDON'S BURNING* you will see that where *TEN IN THE BED* had **two** beats, indicated by/, to the bar, this song has **three**. Thus instead of having one strum for every three syllables or so like *TEN IN THE BED*, *LONDON'S BURNING* has a beat for almost every word. *LONDON'S BURNING* is in what is called **3/4 time**, so that instead of being played with a **one, two, one, two**, rhythm like *TEN IN THE BED*, it is played in a sort of skipping **one, two, three, one, two, three** . . . rhythm.

With this song you must first find that same note D on the 4th string and sing or play the word *LONDON* . . . Your first strum comes on the **syllable** *Burn* . . . the next on the syllable *ing* . . and the third on the syllable *Lon* . . .

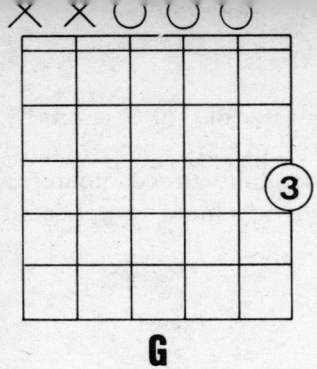

G

HOLD G CHORD

LON-DON'S BURN-ING, LON-DON'S BURN-ING, FETCH THE ENG-INES, FETCH THE ENG-INES, 'FIRE FIRE!' 'FIRE FIRE!' POUR ON WAT-ER, POUR ON WAT-ER

BACK TO START

To show the effect in words:

	London's	BURN	ING	LON don's	BURN	ING	FETCH the
		/	/	/	/	/	/
Hold G Chord		1	2	3	1	2	3

Once again you must keep your strumming to a regular, firm beat, and you should practise until the song and your guitar accompaniment fit together smoothly.

You should really be becoming a master of that G chord by now, so in the next chapter we'll go on to learn another chord in the same key. This will extend your ability to accompany so that you can tackle songs with a slightly more complicated harmonic structure.

THE THREE CHORD TRICK

The two songs you have played so far have both been in the key of G, and you may have noticed that the chord you used to accompany them is also called G, or G Major. G is the **Tonic**, or 'Home Chord', of the key of G. Without going into a lot of complicated musical theory, which is totally unnecessary at this point, this means simply that **any tune in the key of G will use the chord of G a great deal in its accompaniment**. What is more, you can be pretty certain that when it has completed its musical journey the song will end up on the Home Chord of G.

It should now be obvious to you that G is, for the reasons shown above, the most important chord in the key of G. Next to it in importance are the other two **principal chords** of the key, D7 (pronounced D Seventh), and C (or C Major). When these are introduced the harmonic possibilities open to us are increased enormously and we are able to play the accompaniment to a great many more complicated songs. Indeed it has become a standing joke amongst Jazz guitarists that many Pop artists have won fame and fortune with the aid of these three simple chords alone.

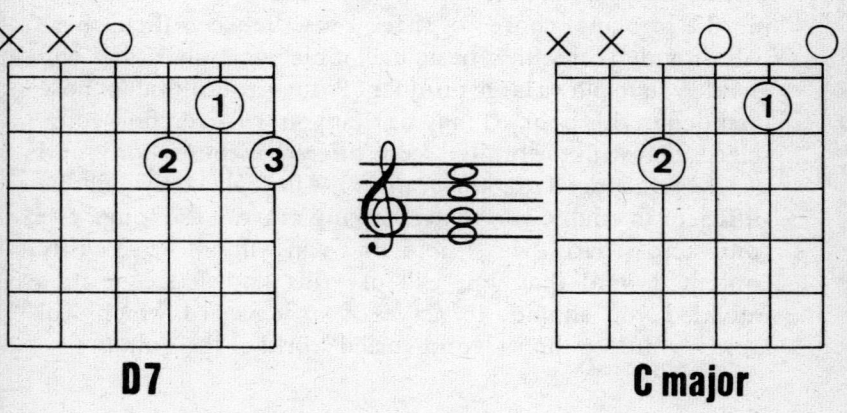

D7   C major

Like many jokes this is something of an exaggeration, but it also has some basis in fact. A large number of early Rock & Roll songs were based on the traditional **12 Bar Blues** chord progression. (A **chord progression** is a set of chords that fit together to form the accompaniment of a song.) And a simple version of the 12 Bar Blues can be played using only the three principal chords of the key. Hence the expression '*The Three Chord Trick*', coined by the understandably envious Jazz players who saw the rich rewards of the commercial field being earned by apparently inferior musicians. Things have changed rather today, because the different styles have merged to such an extent that first class professionals move quite happily from one to the other, which is as it should be. As we have said earlier, the guitar is capable of embracing all kinds of music, so surely the same thing should apply to guitarists.

> You may have noticed that when talking about the 12 Bar Blues chord progression in the paragraph above, I spoke of **the key**, rather than naming the key of G or any other. I did this because **each key** has its three principal chords, which bear the same kind of relationship to each other.

Within the present book we shall confine ourselves to exploring the principal chords of **three** keys. Between them these will provide you with a basic harmonic vocabulary that will enable you to play a large number of songs in addition to those included in this book. It may be that you will even find yourself content with the limited scope offered by these chords and not feel the need to know more. After all, they will be sufficient to enable you to accompany **most** of the songs you come across. However, I hope that you will not be so easily contented, and that you will use this knowledge as it is intended you should, to act as a springboard which will launch you into the rich and varied world of the guitar.

To return to the key of G. Next in importance to the tonic chord G comes D7 (D seventh), and we can say with reasonable certainty that this chord will be contained in the accompaniment of **any song** played in the key of G.

In its simplest four string version, D7 looks like this:

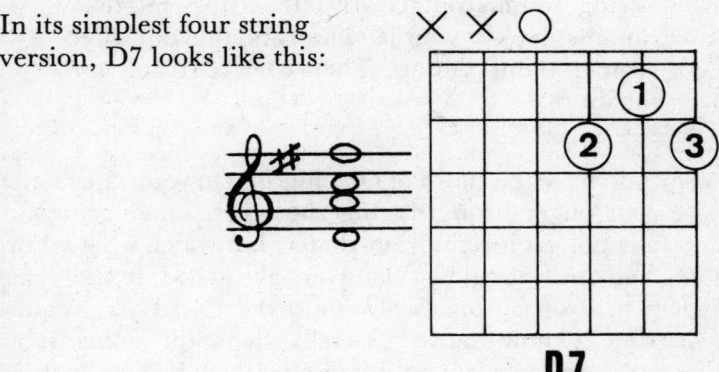

The left hand fingering of this chord is slightly more complicated than that for G Major, so take your time and be sure to use the fingers indicated by the numbers. Note that the 5th and 6th strings have an X above them in the diagram. **Remember that this means they are not sounded in this chord.**

The 4th string has an O above it, indicating that in this chord it is sounded Open, or un-stopped. This means that the only strings you really have to think about are the 3rd, 2nd, and 1st. Look carefully at the Window. Your 2nd finger goes down behind the second fret of the 3rd string. The 1st finger behind the first fret of the 2nd string, and the 3rd finger behind the 2nd fret of the 1st string.

Remember that your thumb should be behind the neck of the instrument, counterbalancing the pressure of your fingers. Now bring your right thumb down across the strings one by one beginning with the 4th, listening to see if each string sounds out clearly. If it doesn't, take another look at your left hand and find out what you're doing wrong. Then correct it and try again.

When you have the chord of D7 sounding to your satisfaction raise your fingers from the fingerboard . . . then try again. You may not get it right immediately but watch what you're doing and think about it. What you have to do is to train your fingers to drop automatically onto the chord you require every time. I know that seems a tall order at the moment, but take my word for it, if you practise you will be able to do it. JUST REMEMBER THAT NOBODY GETS IT RIGHT FIRST TIME WITHOUT EFFORT. That's what practice is for, to run through your quota of mistakes, so that next time you and your fingers know better.

Now, if you feel quite happy about your D7, try moving from that chord back to G, strumming across the strings again with your thumb. You will find that this move sounds logical, as if the two chords are related. This is as it should be. A D7 **usually** moves to a G Major when you are playing in the key of G. This is a natural harmonic progression.

Do this change a number of times. At first you'll find it necessary to look down at the fingerboard and guide your left hand fingers carefully into position. Don't worry if this seems awkward to you. We've all been through this stage, and the only way to get past it is to practise the change again and again until you are able to make it smoothly every time. Don't try to do it too quickly. Speed will come naturally with time. Accuracy is more important, because what you should be practising is **doing it right**.

So now you have two chords in your repertoire, G and D7, and you should be ready to tackle a slightly more complicated tune which uses both of these chords: *OH, DEAR, WHAT CAN THE MATTER BE?*

This song is in 3 to the bar Waltz rhythm, so it might be a good idea to try a slight variation in your right hand. Instead of strumming straight across the top four strings with your thumb, this time use your thumb only to pluck the 4th string and your three fingers in their natural positions on the top three strings. The idea is to play the first beat of the bar on the 4th string with your thumb, and the second two on the top three strings by plucking all three together sideways and slightly upwards as shown in the diagram. Remember to keep the thumb well forward or it will get in the way of your fingers.

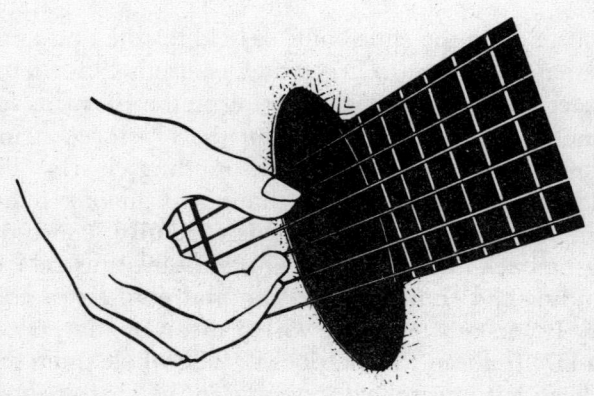

Try doing this with the G chord at first, as an exercise before you attempt the tune itself. This will enable you to concentrate on getting your right hand action as smooth and natural as possible. Count *One, Two, Three — Thumb, Fingers, Fingers.* Try this a number of times, then finger the D7 chord with your left hand and repeat the exercise.

OH, DEAR, WHAT CAN THE MATTER BE?

Now to begin *OH, DEAR, WHAT CAN THE MATTER BE?* The first note is D, which you will find on the third fret of your 2nd string. And the second note is the same, so that the words *OH, DEAR* are both D'S. Each of these is sung to a count of 1, 2, 3. So whilst you are singing *OH*, your accompaniment actually plays three beats which sound **um, ching, ching**. The same thing applies for the second bar, where the word of the song is *DEAR*, behind which you again play **um, ching, ching**. After that, the melody begins to move around more, following the beat, but you still stay on the chord of G. This, of course, is one of the reasons that it is easier to play a chordal accompaniment than actually playing the melody — because chords often stay in the same place whilst the melody is jumping around.

So, in this song the chord of G is held for the first four bars. After that you move to D7, which is also held for four bars. You keep on using the open D string on the 4th string for your bass note, although the notes on the top three strings are changed. Make sure they're all sounding clearly! The rest should be plain sailing — just changing from one to the other of your two chords, and **note this carefully**, concluding by changing back from D7 to G. This ends the musical journey, concluding the chord progression and giving it a complete sound. If you're wondering what I mean by that, try ending up on D7. It doesn't work, does it? The whole thing seems to have been left unresolved, hanging in the air somehow.

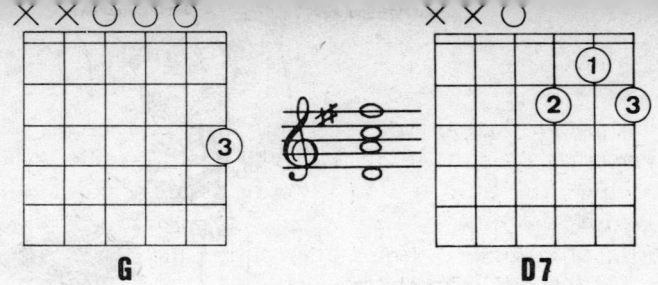

G

CHORUS: OH DEAR! WHAT CAN THE MAT-TER BE?

D7

DEAR DEAR! WHAT CAN THE MAT-TER BE?

G

OH DEAR! WHAT CAN THE MATTER BE?

D7   **G**

JOHN-NY'S SO LONG AT THE FAIR.   VERSE: HE

PROM-ISED TO BUY ME A BUNCH OF BLUE RIB-BONS, HE

D7

PROM-ISED TO BUY ME A BUNCH OF BLUE RIB-BONS, HE

G

PROM-ISED TO BUY ME A BUNCH OF BLUE RIB-BONS, TO

D7   **G**

TIE UP MY BON-NY BROWN HAIR.

BONNY BOBBY SHAFTO

Fine! Now to get you even more used to these two chords we'll have another song which uses them, *BOBBY SHAFTO*. This one is in Four Four time, which means that you should count 1, 2, 3, 4 to the bar, but let's try using the thumb and fingers type of accompaniment again. This time it will be slightly different, of course, so that your thumb will come on the 1st and 3rd beats of the bar, and your fingers on the 2nd and 4th.

The rhythm you are playing will be **um, ching, um, ching** or **Thumb, Fingers, Thumb, Fingers**. And the melody will be jumping around in time with it for a lot of the song. The main thing to make sure of here, as with all accompaniment playing, is that you keep up a regular rhythm throughout.

The first three notes of the song, corresponding to the words, *BOBBY SHAFT*, are all Gs, the same note as your open 3rd string.

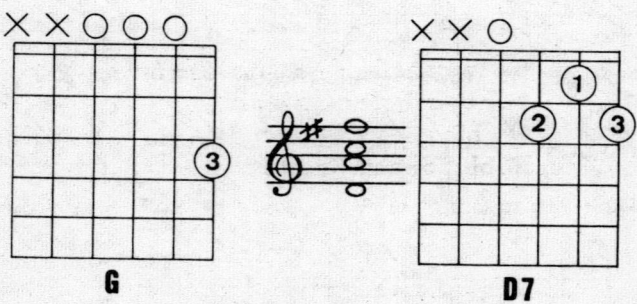

G   D7

BONNY BOBBY SHAFTO

Thumb Fingers Thumb Fingers T F T F etc.

Bobby Shafto's tall and slim
He's dressed up so neat and trim
The lassies always look at him
Bonny Bobby Shafto.

Chorus

Bobby Shafto's gett'n a bairn
For to dangle on his airm
On his airm and on his knee
Bobby Bobby Shafto

PERFORMING THE TRICK

So far we have learned to use the chords of G and D7. This only leaves the third principal chord in the key of G, which is, as mentioned earlier named C, or C Major.

C Major looks like this in its four string version:

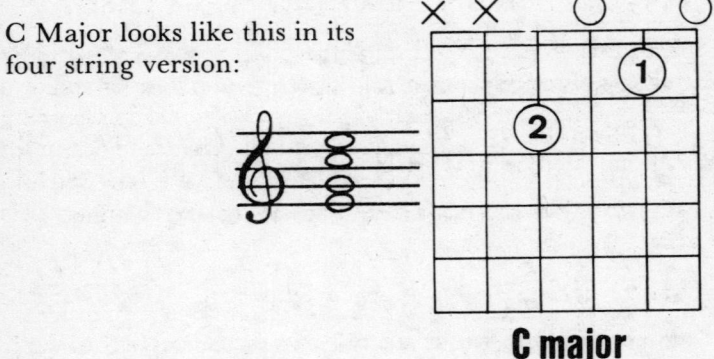

C major

Note the X symbols over the Nut position, which tell you that the 5th and 6th strings are not sounded in this chord. Once again, the O above the 1st and 3rd strings indicates that they should be sounded open, or un-fingered. Your first finger goes down behind the first fret of the 2nd string, and your second behind the second fret on the 4th string. Make sure you are using the correct fingers and placing them in the right position — **just behind the frets**. Then strum across those top four strings with your right hand thumb.

Are all the notes sounding? If they're not, check up as explained previously to make sure that none of your left hand fingers are overlapping or catching on another string, and that the first and second fingers are pressing the strings down so that they make a firm good contact with the frets.

Whilst your left hand is in this position, with your 1st and 2nd fingers occupied, take a look and find out what the other fingers, your 3rd and 4th are doing. Chances are that the 4th finger in particular is sticking out almost at right angles to the fingerboard, with the 3rd doing something similar. Added to this there is probably quite a lot of unnecessary tension in your left hand because you're pressing down like grim death on those fingers which are actually fretting the strings.

Are you? Of course you are! Now I want you to make a deliberate effort to **relax** that hand, so that you are only using just enough pressure with the 1st and 2nd fingers to maintain a clear note on the strings they are fretting. And your 3rd and 4th fingers, **which aren't actually doing anything in this chord** — well, I want you to give them a little holiday.

> Allow them to **relax** and droop
> down towards the fingerboard,
> coming as near to it as they
> can without actually touching
> the strings.

You may not get the point of what I'm telling you above for quite a time, but **believe me** I wish there had been someone around to tell me about this when I was at your stage of learning to play the guitar. As you will have already begun to appreciate, the fingers of your left hand play a **very** important part in guitar playing. They are the ones which actually determine the notes you are playing — either as single notes or as chords. As you progress they will be called upon to perform more and more complex patterns of movement up and down and across the fingerboard. Therefore, it is desirable that your fingers should remain at all times as close to the strings as possible. That way they will have a smaller distance to travel in order to do their job, and moving a small distance is naturally quicker than a large one.

I said earlier that there is no Golden Key to guitar playing, but I have to admit that the principles **Economy of Movement** and **Relaxation** come very close to being something like that. If you make an effort to follow these principles now they will make things much easier for you later on.

Now that we've completed the Three Chord Trick in the Key of G let's take another look at the three chords involved:

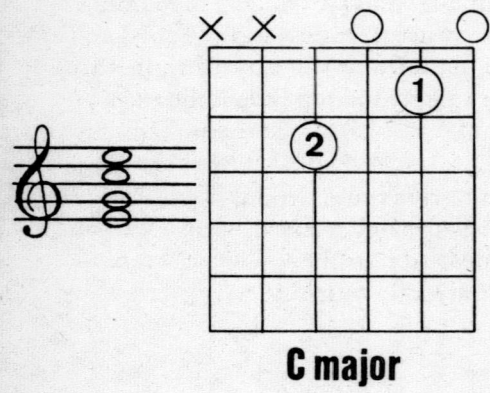

C major

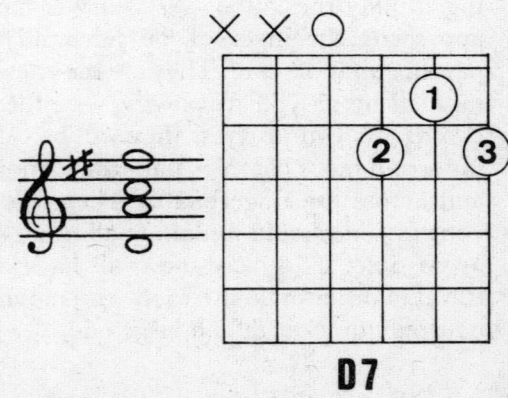

D7

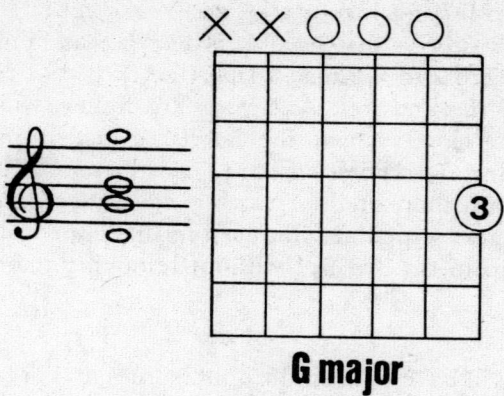

G major

You will notice that the three chords are shown in the reverse order from the way in which you have learned them. This has been done because played in this way they form a **cadence, or progression,** which is complete in itself. It sounds right, moving logically and ending on the Tonic, or home chord of G. Now I would like you to play the three chords, moving from one to the other as shown below.

//: **C***//* | **D7***//* | **G***//* :*//*

There you have three bars in 3/4 time — the bars consisting of three beats are indicated by the upright lines. You should strum the chords with your thumb, counting *1 . . . 2 . . . 3 . . ., 1 . . . 2 . . . 3 . . .,* etc. The chord symbol itself counts as one beat, and each of the diagonal lines (/) which follow count as one beat each. So you can see that in this example each chord is played three times.

Make your beat a regular one, but go as slowly as you like at first, concentrating on making the changes as smoothly as possible, thinking about what you're doing. When you move from the C to D7, for instance — don't take your 1st finger off the 2nd string — just leave it where it was. Your 2nd finger slips across to the next string (the 3rd), but remains close behind the 2nd fret. And your 3rd finger, which has been hanging closely above the 1st string just drops down behind the 2nd fret. Then for the G chord — well your 3rd finger is already there on the 1st string, **so releasing your 1st and 2nd fingers which are not used in this chord**, slide the 3rd finger up to the 3rd fret without removing it from the string at all.

You will have noticed the double lines and dots //:   :// enclosing the chords in the notation above. This is a way of indicating a **Repeat**. Everything between those double lines is repeated. So, when you've moved through the three chords, just go back to the beginning and start again . . with no break. This sort of repetition is very good practice, because you will find that your fingers start to change their positions smoothly and almost automatically.

I should add a word of warning here. When you practise — DO IT ALONE. Practice is a very private business, and it is something quite distinct from playing in front of other people. To anybody listening, practice, **real practice** would sound monotonous and boring. By repeating the Three Chord Trick over and over again in the same key you could probably drive the rest of the family mad if you do it somewhere where they can't avoid listening to you.

It isn't, or shouldn't be, monotonous to **you** because you're concentrating on what you're doing and there's always a lot to think about, especially in these early stages. You should be listening to the sound you are making. ALWAYS LISTEN.

Are the notes sounding clearly? If not, are each of your fingers placed correctly? So, find somewhere where you can practise out of earshot of other people. And if they ask to hear what you're doing, tell them that you'll let them know when you're ready to perform.

> **And when you do perform — only play what you really know and are confident of**. People will enjoy what you play much more if you are sure of what you are doing and don't make too many mistakes. And you will find that **you** will enjoy it more too!

Now, having practised the three Principal chords of G on their own, let's use them in a song. *TEN GREEN BOTTLES* is another word game like *TEN IN THE BED*..

TEN GREEN BOTTLES

The syllables *TEN GREEN BOT* are all on the note G, which is the same as your open 3rd string, so perhaps you'd like to find that for a start. The rhythm here is 4 to the bar, as indicated by the diagonal strokes (/) — remember that the chord symbol itself counts as one beat as well. Take it slowly and steadily at first, because you'll find that several times in this song you are called on to change a chord in the middle of a bar. Thus in the 2nd and 4th bars you have only **two** beats on D7 before moving to G. Similarly in the 5th bar you have to move from C to G after only two beats. It doesn't matter if those green bottles seem to fall rather slowly at first, just concentrate on getting those changes smoothly. By the time you get to *No Green Bottles* you should really be getting to be familiar with the chords of G. Just to prove that this is so, here's one more song which will reinforce that knowledge.

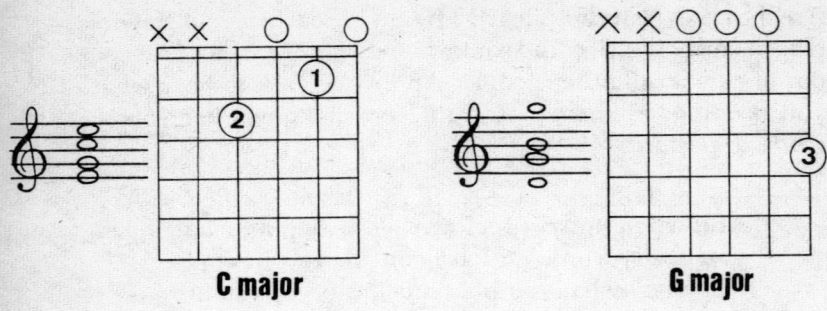

C major

G major

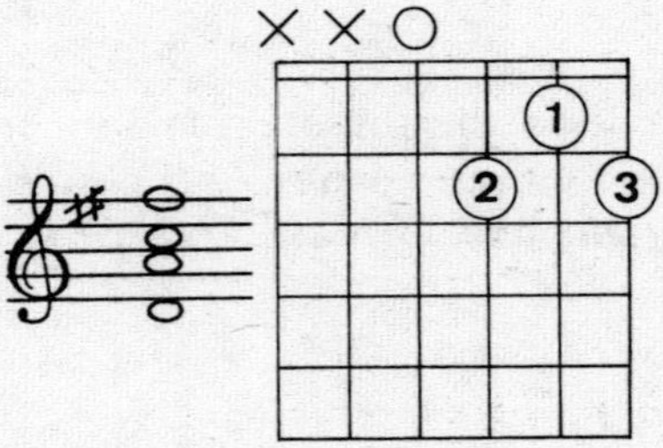

D7

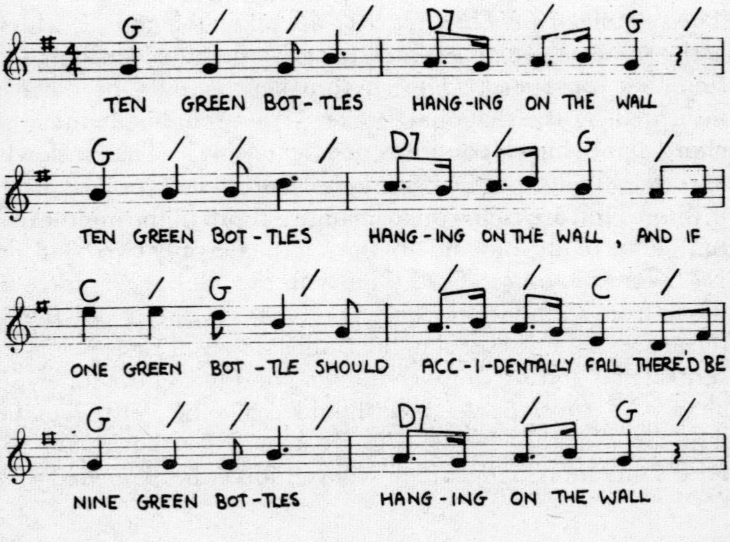

G D7 G
TEN GREEN BOT-TLES HANG-ING ON THE WALL
G D7 G
TEN GREEN BOT-TLES HANG-ING ON THE WALL, AND IF
C G C
ONE GREEN BOT-TLE SHOULD ACC-I-DENTALLY FALL THERE'D BE
G D7 G
NINE GREEN BOT-TLES HANG-ING ON THE WALL

CHORDS IN D MAJOR

Our next, most logical move from the guitar playing point of view is into the Key of D. This means that the chord of D becomes our Tonic or Home chord, the one which will be played quite a lot throughout the song and almost inevitably as the last chord.

In its easiest form the chord of D Major looks like this:

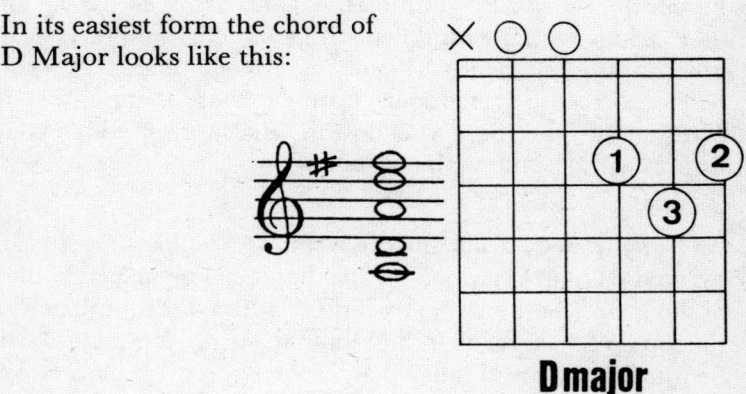

D major

The 6th string is not sounded in this version of the chord, and therefore carries the symbol X above it in the window. However, the 4th and 5th strings can be sounded Open, and will give the chord a ringing, sonorous sound.

As you may already have guessed the chord D Major is a close relative of the D7 which you have learned already — a kind of reverse image of it, in fact, where the triangular pattern of the fingers is turned upside down. Now is a good time to begin recognising these patterns on the fingerboard, because chords are in effect just that.

The fact that the pattern is reversed in this case means that the fingers used have to be changed, so that now it is the 1st finger which frets the 3rd string at the 2nd fret and the 2nd finger on the 1st string at the same fret. The 3rd finger goes down there on the 3rd fret of the 2nd string.

Your fingers may feel a bit crowded at first, but you will find that D is an easy chord to play once you have got used to it. Finger the chord with your left hand and strum across the top four strings with a firm down stroke of your thumb. Is each note ringing out clearly? If not, see if your fingers are positioned correctly. If necessary, you can raise them and start over again. The more you do this, the more familiar your fingers will become with the pattern.

As I mentioned earlier the 5th string (A) is, like the 4th (D) marked with an O, which means that it can be played as part of the chord. So now try strumming with your thumb across the top **five** strings, including that 5th string. The sound will be much louder and fuller than before.

The open 4th and 5th strings provide what are known as the **Bass** notes of the D chord. They will give a foundation of low notes on which your accompaniment can be built. Try plucking downwards with your thumb on the 4th string, followed by the 5th string. Then go back to the 4th string, the 5th . . . and so on, repeating the pattern of the two notes. D . . . A . . . D . . . A . . . and so on, in a regular, heartbeat rhythm.

Remember that your thumb should be well forward of your right hand fingers, and moving at the second joint.

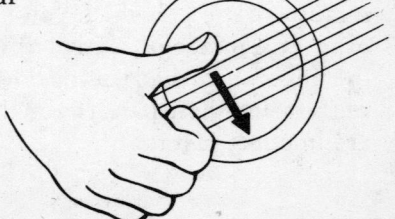

Once you have the idea of using your
thumb in this way, finger the D chord
with your left hand and after plucking
the bass note with your thumb brush
down with the back of your index
finger across the top three strings
instead of using one right hand finger
for each of them.

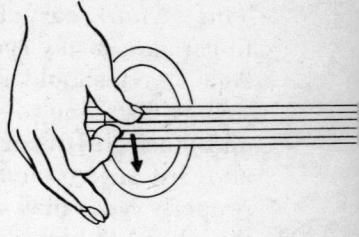

You will find that this produces a different kind of sound,
because instead of being plucked by the fleshy part of the
fingers the strings are set in motion by the **nail** of the index
finger. This produces a brighter, more percussive tone, and it
is indeed an elaboration of this kind of technique that the
Flamenco players use to produce their tremendous rhythmic
patterns.

STRING	4		5	
	D		A	
	P	i	P	i
		↓		↓

Now that you've got the idea of D Major, the next most
important chord in the key is A7, or A Seventh.

Your 2nd finger goes down
just behind the 2nd fret on the
fourth string, while the 3rd
finger should be behind the
2nd fret of the second string.

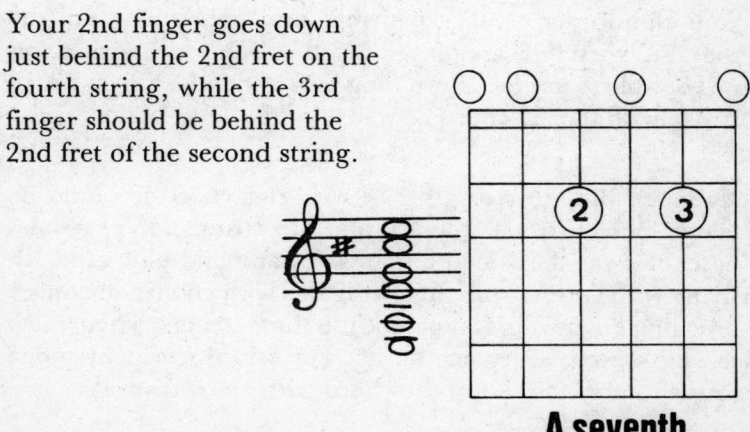

A seventh

This is a fairly easy chord to finger because your fingers are nicely spaced, on alternate strings. Again you should strum across the top four strings, listening to see that every note is clear and musical. If your fingers are fouling the 1st and 3rd strings and stopping them sounding properly you may find that your left hand thumb is too high on the back of the neck and should be nearer to the centre, as in the diagram.

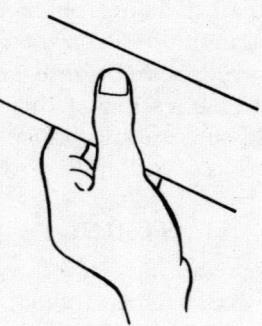

Looking at the chord window for A7 you will see that **none** of the strings has an X symbol above it. **All** the strings which are not actually fretted have the O above them, so this time draw your thumb across all **six** strings and notice how full the sound is when they are played together. This means that you will be able to use the alternating bass and index finger brush stroke with the A7 chord as well as with the D Major.

Although the 6th string fits in with this chord it would be better for you to use the 4th and 5th strings for your bass notes. Finger the A7 with your left hand and pluck the 4th string with your thumb, following this with your index finger brushing downwards across the top three strings. Then pluck the 5th string with your thumb, and again use your index finger to play the rest of the chord with a down stroke.

When you fret the 4th string at the
2nd fret in this way it means that it is
sounding as the note E — so your
thumb and finger stroke is shown like
this:

STRING	4	3	5	3
	(E)	2	(A)	2
		1		1
	Thumb	Index	Thumb	Index
		↓		↓

You may be having difficulty with your thumb at this point
not always hitting the right string. This is quite normal.
Repetition and thoughtful, slow practice will eventually
enable your thumb to find its way to the right string every
time.

We shall be using the two new chords D and A7 in a song
before long, but first let's practise changing from one to the
other bearing in mind the principal of Economy of Movement
which we talked about earlier. If you look at the use of your
fingers in these two chords you will find that the 3rd finger
need not leave the 2nd string. In the D chord it is behind the
3rd fret on the 2nd string, in the A7 behind the 2nd fret. So, if
you are going from D to A7 you move it **down** one fret, or
from A7 to D you move it **up** one fret. Your 1st finger is not
used in the A7, and when changing from D to A7 your 2nd
finger simply hops over from the 2nd fret of the 1st string to
the 2nd fret, 3rd string.

Try changing between the two chords,
using down strokes with your thumb.

| |: **D**/// | **A7**/// | **D**/// :| |

Now we come to a simple little song which you are sure to
know, called *POLLY WOLLY DOODLE*.

POLLY WOLLY DOODLE

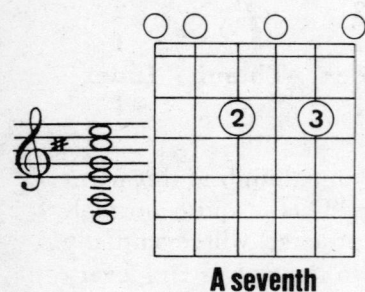

A seventh

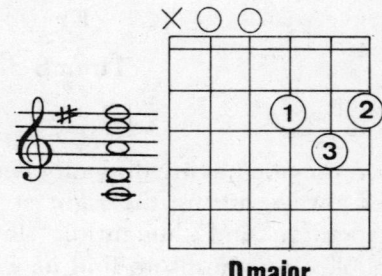

D major

(Thumb) (Brush) (Thumb) (Brush)
p   i   p   i   etc.

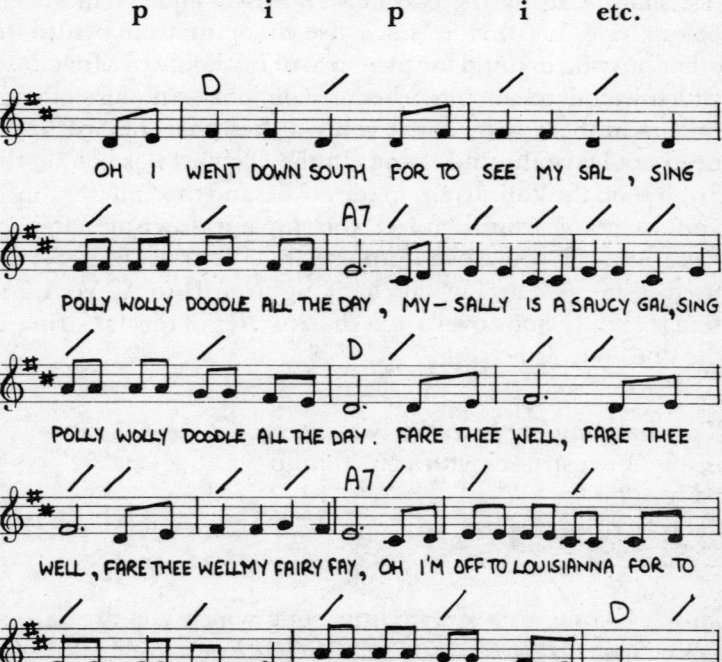

OH I WENT DOWN SOUTH FOR TO SEE MY SAL , SING

POLLY WOLLY DOODLE ALL THE DAY , MY—SALLY IS A SAUCY GAL, SING

POLLY WOLLY DOODLE ALL THE DAY . FARE THEE WELL, FARE THEE

WELL , FARE THEE WELL MY FAIRY FAY, OH I'M OFF TO LOUISIANNA FOR TO

SEE MY SUSY ANNA, SING POLLY WOLLY DOODLE ALL THE DAY.

If you look at the chords and words of this song you will see that it starts with a D chord, changing to an A7 on *DAY* through again to *DAY*. Although you can accompany the song with thumb strokes on *WENT* . . . *SOUTH* . . . *SEE* . . . etc. (that is **two** beats to the bar), you will be able to play a much more suitable accompaniment if you use the thumb and finger brush stroke we have been talking about in this chapter.

(Thumb) (Brush) (Thumb) (Brush)
    p   **i**   **p**   **i**   **etc.**

The third Principal chord in the Key of D Major is G Major. This is one you already know and have been using in all the songs up to now as the Tonic, or Home chord. It has a slightly different function in the key of D Major, but still an important one because the keys are so closely related, and you will find it occurring frequently in songs in D Major.

Because you are already familiar with the G chord we can now go on to try a fuller version of it which uses all six strings.

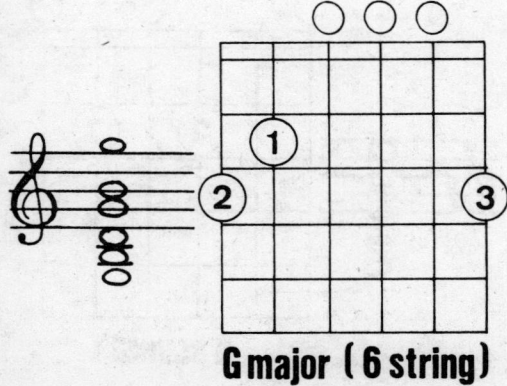

G major (6 string)

If you look at the numbers in the diagram you will see that your 1st finger is placed behind the 2nd fret on the 5th string and your 2nd finger behind the 3rd fret on the 6th string. **The 3rd finger** remains on the 1st string; where it was originally. You may find the stretch difficult at first. Make sure that your left hand thumb is at the **centre** of the back of the neck and that none of your fingers are touching strings next to the ones they are fretting. Draw your thumb slowly across all six strings and listen to them one by one.

You now have all three of the principal chords of D Major.

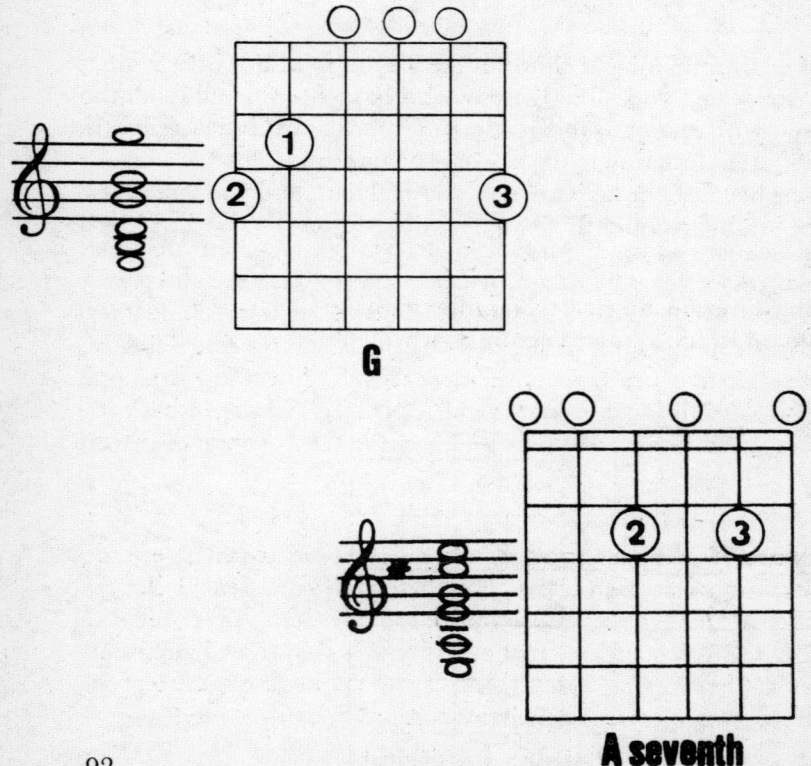

G

A seventh

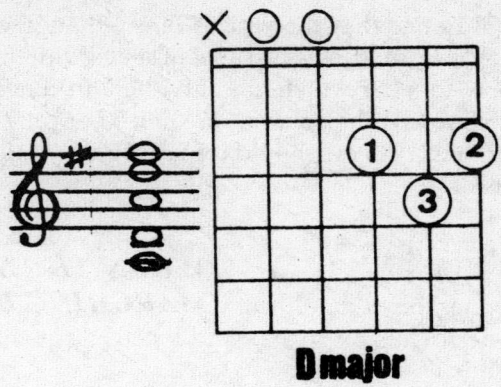

D major

Now, beginning as slowly as you like, play through these chords as indicated below, using down strokes of the thumb

| |: **D**/// | **G**/// | **A7**/// | **D**/// :| |

Once again, remember that double lines and dots mean that the chords within them should be repeated, so when you reach the end of the progression go back to the beginning and play it over and over. Make sure every chord is getting its full value, that every note is sounding, and that you are playing a steady, regular rhythm. If you find any difficulty in getting from one chord to another, stop, think about it, and examine what your left hand fingers are doing. Then try that change over and over by itself.

Now, if you're happy about those three chords, let's go straight ahead and learn another song which uses all three of them. This is a real old favourite called *WHEN THE SAINTS GO MARCHING IN*. It should be played in a lively manner, and in this instance you could try using just the thumb of the right hand playing four beats to the bar as indicated.

You will notice that the chords don't change very often, so you should be able to get up a bit of speed with this one. When you come to a bar which has only the four diagonal lines //// and **no** chord symbol, as with the first 6 bars of *THE SAINTS*, your left hand fingers should remain on the same chord — **in this case D**.

WHEN THE SAINTS GO MARCHING IN

D major

OH WHEN THE SAINTS GO MARCH-ING IN

OH WHEN THE SAINTS GO MARCH-ING IN

OH I WANT TO BE IN THAT NUM-BER

WHEN THE SAINTS GO MARCH-ING IN.

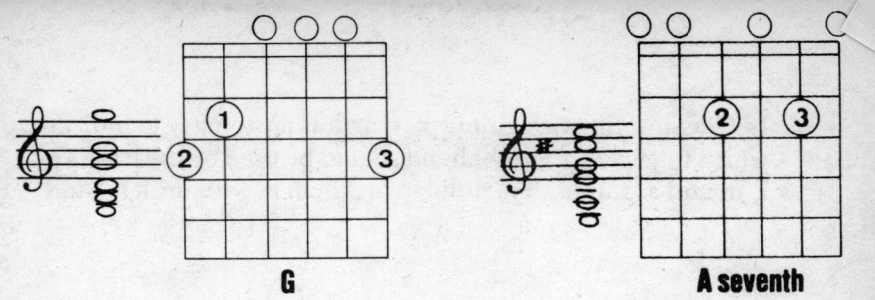

G

A seventh

Additional words:

And when the sun begins to shine
When that sun begins to shine
Oh I want to be in that number
When the sun begins to shine.

When the band begins to play . . . etc.

When that trumpet sounds a call . . . etc.

In this song the melody picks up on the second beat of the first bar, so that you have to count a silent ONE, followed by the words *OH, WHEN THE*, which make up the remaining three beats of that bar.

The first note of the melody is on your Open 4th string, followed by the 4th fret, 4th string, then by the Open 3rd.

OH	*WHEN*	*THE*
D	**F#**	**G**

The F is sharpened — i.e. on the 4th fret rather than the 3rd as you might expect, because the song is in the key of D. I'm not going to go into explaining why that is so at the moment, because in this book we are concentrating on the physical task of playing the guitar, rather than on musical theory.

In Classical Spanish guitar playing it is customary to indicate which fingers of the right hand should be used by the letters **p, i, m and a**, rather than numbering them as with the left hand.

p i m a

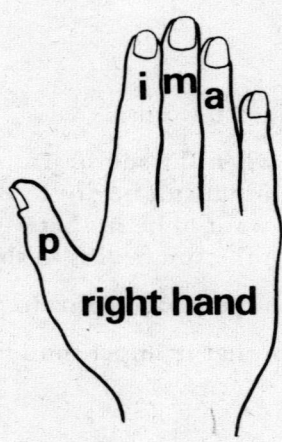

The letters are derived from the Spanish names for the fingers, as shown below:

1st finger = **i**, from *Indice*, Index.

2nd finger = **m**, from *medio*, Middle.

3rd finger = **a**, from *Anular*, or Ring finger.

Thumb = **p**, from *Pulgar*, Thumb.

Under this system a thumb strum would be shown as:

//:**G**///\   **D7**///\   **G**///://
  PPPP   PPPP   PPPP

Or a 3 to the bar rhythm like that of *OH, DEAR, WHAT CAN THE MATTER BE?* would be written as:

```
||:      G/  /  |  G/  /  :||

         p i  i      p i  i
           m m          m m
           a a          a a
```

Another means of producing a sharp, percussive rhythm is by the use of a **plectrum**, which is a piece of plastic, bone or shell, held between the 1st finger and thumb of the right hand.

A plectrum will produce a brighter and louder sound than the fingers, BUT it is not normally used on a Nylon strung guitar. Its original use was on the steel strung acoustic guitar, to play rhythms in a dance band before the days of amplification. For this purpose as much volume and cutting power as possible were essential. Today a number of Folk players will vary their playing by the occasional use of a plectrum, and it is of course used by Electric guitarists to play either single string solos or rhythm.

The plectrum is very useful, but later on when you come to consider the possibilities of un-accompanied solo playing you may decide, as I did, to abandon it in favour of the fingers,

MORE ABOUT THE RIGHT HAND

Whilst your left hand is occupied with fingering chordal patterns, your right is the one which actually provides the motive power and makes the sound. Dealing as we are in this book solely with song accompaniment, it follows that your use of the right hand is extremely important from several points of view, not the least of which is the provision of a regular beat, or rhythm.

There are any number of different rhythms, and a large number of ways in which they can be produced on the guitar. If you want to see and hear something really spectacular you should watch a good Spanish Flamenco player performing a Rhumba rhythm.

Not only does he make a tremendous rhythmic sound with the strings of the guitar, but he will at the same time be tapping the body, so that the total effect is one of several drums and guitars playing at the same time.

I don't expect your playing to be quite up to that standard yet, of course. But let's examine some of the different methods of producing a rhythmic accompaniment on the guitar. So far you have used three basic methods.

98

First the down stroke of the
thumb strumming across the
strings:

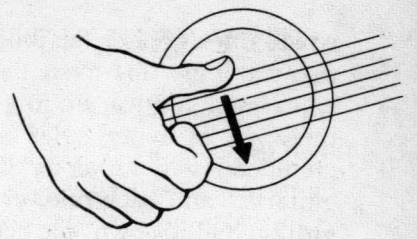

Then you used your thumb on
the bass strings and one each
of your fingers for the top
three strings:

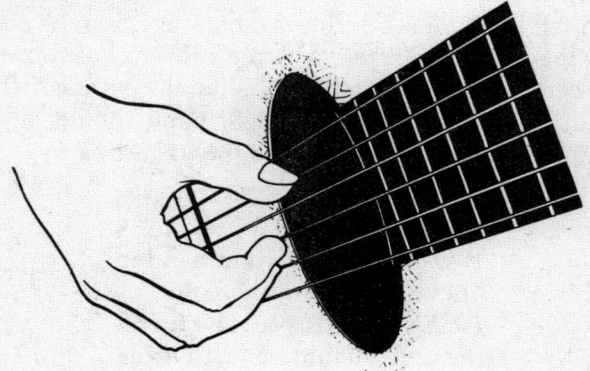

The third method was to use
the thumb on the bass strings
again, but to sound the other
strings by striking them with
the back, and hence the nail,
of your Index finger,
producing a somewhat sharper
tone.

which offer greater flexibility in many respects. As with so many things, this must be a matter of personal taste and experimentation in finding **your own style** of playing, and there are as many styles as there are guitarists. I recently attended a seminar along with twenty-five other experienced guitarists and each one, **even if he was playing the same guitar**, had his own, particular distinctive sound.

To return to the use of the right hand fingers, I must make it clear at this point that the fingernails of your right hand are one of your most important assets as a guitarist and you should do your best to take good care of them. Whilst the nails of your left hand must be trimmed back as closely as possible, so that they do not interfere with the efficiency of your fingering by catching on the strings and generally getting in the way of clean fretting, those of the right hand should be rather longer, extending slightly beyond the fingertips.

If you hold your right hand up at eye level, with the palm facing towards you, the tip of the nails should be just visible. They should not overtop the fingertips by more than one millimetre and should match their individual shape.

Any necessary adjustment in the length and shape of your nails must be carried out with the utmost care. They should never be trimmed with scissors, but with a good quality diamond-cut file, and afterwards they should be polished with a leather buffer to make sure that they are **perfectly** smooth. Any unevenness or jagged edges will interfere with the nail's contact with the string and affect the quality of sound produced.

If you are in the habit of biting your nails, you have no doubt been told many times that you **shouldn't** so I'm not going to bore you by repeating that instruction. What I would say is that **if you must bite them** bite only on the **left** hand, where they should be short anyway. Some people's nails are naturally stronger than others. Just why this is so, nobody seems entirely certain, neither have they come up with an infallible remedy for strengthening weak nails. However you might like to try Nick's solution, which is **to eat lots of wobbly jelly**!

Don't attempt to play with the nails **only**. If you are able to do this your nails are almost certainly too long, and in any case the sound you make will be too metallic. The string is struck first with the tip of the finger, swiftly followed by the nail edge, which glides quickly past it adding sharpness and definition. The skin of the finger-tip alone is not sufficient to produce the tone and volume required, although it will harden in time and help improve your tone.

Now let's get back to really **using** the right hand fingers. When a song is slow moving and melodic in its content you will find it effective to use an *arpeggio* style of accompaniment. *Arpeggio* is derived from the Italian term for a Harp. Thus *arpeggio* accompaniment provides a harp-like sound, with the notes of a chord played one after the other, rather than all at the same time in more rhythmic accompaniments, and allowed to ring.

Take your simple 4 string G Major chord and try it in this way.

Place your right hand thumb
close to the 4th (D string) and
position the fingers with the
1st against the 3rd string, the
2nd against the 2nd string and
the 3rd against the 1st.

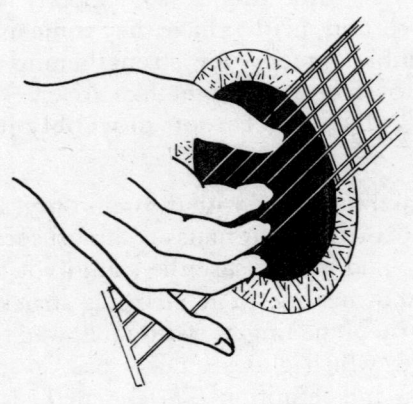

Now hit downwards on the D string
with your thumb, then follow that
with your fingers, one by one,
commencing with the 1st, plucking
upwards on the 3rd, 2nd, and 1st
respectively.

In Spanish guitar notation that would look like this:

p i m a   p i m a . . . . etc.

When playing this kind of accompaniment you should still maintain some kind of a regular beat, by trying to make the sound of each string equal in length and counting, if only sub-consciously, 1 . . . 2 . . . 3 . . . 4 . . . If you don't, instead of being merely relaxed and fluid, the whole thing may tend to drag and lose any sense of coherence.

Now, you may remember — I hope you do! — that the very first chord we played on the Open 6th, 3rd, 2nd and 1st strings was E Minor (Em), and it looked like this:

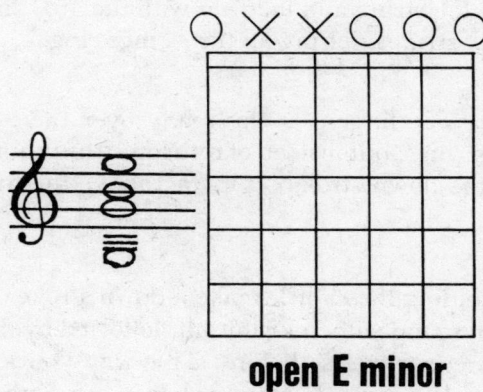

open E minor

You've moved quite a way ahead in your guitar playing since then, so now let's take another look at E Minor, but this time a complete and much fuller sounding version, like this:

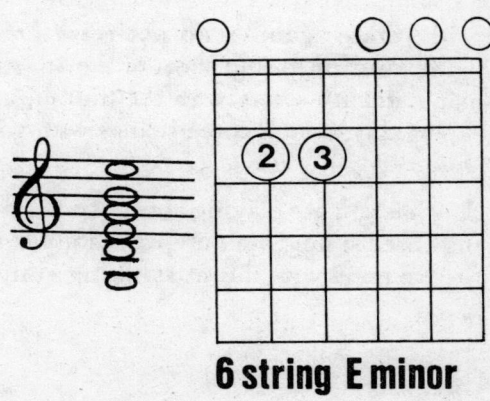

6 string E minor

Simple enough to finger with your left hand, isn't it? Just the 2nd and 3rd fingers, placed firmly down behind the 2nd fret on the 5th and 4th strings respectively.

Now, once you've done that put your right hand thumb next to the 6th string and your 1st, 2nd and 3rd fingers one each on the top strings as before.

Now make a downward stroke with your thumb on the 6th string and follow it with the 3rd, 2nd and 1st strings, letting all the strings ring.

Leave your fingers at the ready over the top three strings, but instead of returning the thumb after the down stroke let it stay above the **5th string**.

Still holding the chord, make a down stroke on the 5th string with your thumb, followed by the top three strings as before. This way you are playing the same E Minor chord, but with a different bass note — and letting it ring, of course, in *arpeggio* fashion.

Once again — **do not return the thumb**, but allow it to stop short of the 4th string. Then hit the 4th string with the thumb, and once again play the top three strings with your fingers.

So what you are playing above is a **p i m a** right hand fingering **three times**, the only variation being that on each of the three **p** notes your thumb is hitting a different string, like this:

(E Minor Chord throughout)

STRING	6	3	2	1	5	3	2	1	4	3	2	1
FINGER	p	i	m	a	p	i	m	a	p	i	m	a

Each one of these is an equally valid E Minor chord *arpeggio*, but each has its own characteristic sound. Thus, although the chord of an accompaniment does not change, it is still possible to add variety and colour by varying the bass note in this way. I'd like you to experiment with this for yourself, remembering always to keep those fingers over the top three strings, alternating the bass notes and listening to the sound you are making.

Minor chords are particularly effective on the guitar, giving a wonderful feeling of drama and mystery. Something else you might like to try with this chord formation is a very simple form of *arpeggio*, which can be obtained by drawing just your thumb alone slowly across all six strings and letting them ring. This is an effect that will only work when the chord involved is a six string one, of course.

The other chord I want to introduce to you in this chapter is that of A Minor, and it looks like this:

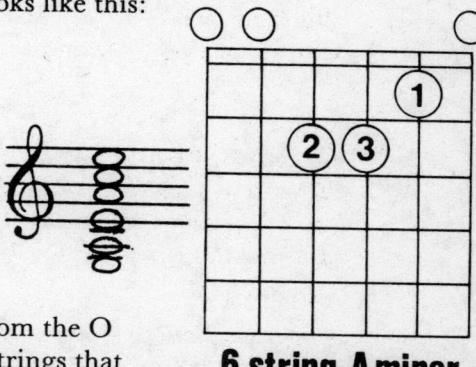

6 string A minor

Once again you will see from the O over the 1st, 5th and 6th strings that this is a six string chord, and not too difficult to finger if you follow the numbers shown in the diagram.

Here again, with the two open bass strings you have a full-sounding, sonorous chord, and I would like you to try playing it *arpeggio* fashion in the same way as you did with E Minor, using the **p i m a** fingering with your right hand and varying the bass note in the same way.

When you're happy about the Left hand fingering take the two chords together and play *arpeggios* on the one after the other. You will notice that when you change from **Em** to **Am** your 2nd and 3rd Left hand fingers retain the same shape in relation to each other. They simply move from the 5th and 4th strings to the 4th and 3rd strings, while your 1st finger pressed down behind the 1st fret on the second string.

To finish off this chapter, and to give you more experience with the use of *arpeggio* accompaniment here is a rather special song which uses both major and minor chords and lends itself particularly to this style.

OVER THE SEA TO SKYE

In your previous *arpeggio* practice you have been playing **p a m i** with your right hand, which is four notes in all, implying a four beat bar. *OVER THE SEA TO SKYE* however is in 3/4 time, so we shall have to modify the form of our original *arpeggio* slightly. The best way of doing this will be to split up the 3 beats of the bar into 6 and to play the same chord with a **p i m a m i** pattern, which will look as shown below:

STRING	6	3	2	1	2	3
FINGER	**p**	**i**	**m**	**a**	**m**	**i**

Before you try to play the song itself, take the chord shapes one by one and practise the kind of picking pattern shown above. Once again you can begin as slowly as you like, and concentrate on the **sound** making sure that every string is ringing as it should. When you have the pattern in your mind and fingers try varying the bass notes by moving your thumb to the 5th then the 4th strings. As I mentioned above, the beauty of this when you're dealing with six string chords is that **whatever string you hit** you're not going to play any wrong notes, because all the notes of the chord will fit.

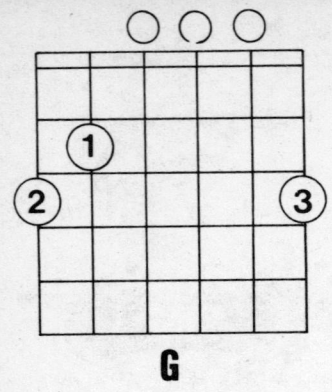

G

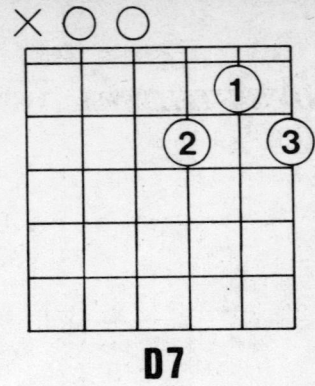

D7

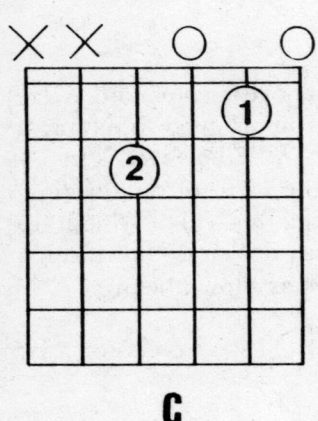

C

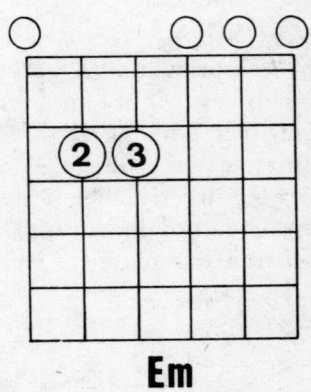

Em

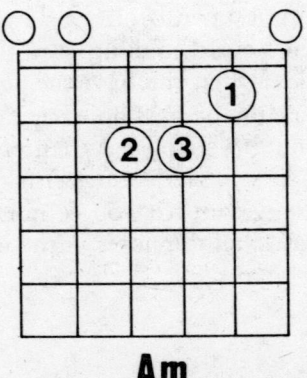

Am

OVER THE SEA TO SKYE

CHORDS IN C MAJOR

Our next key of C Major is used a great deal in song accompaniments. It is closely related to the key of G, and its Tonic, or Home chord is naturally C Major. You have already learned this as one of the principal chords of key of G. The other two important chords are G7 (G Seventh) and F (F Major.).

You have only learned a four string version of C so far, so now let's extend that to a six string chord, which looks like this:

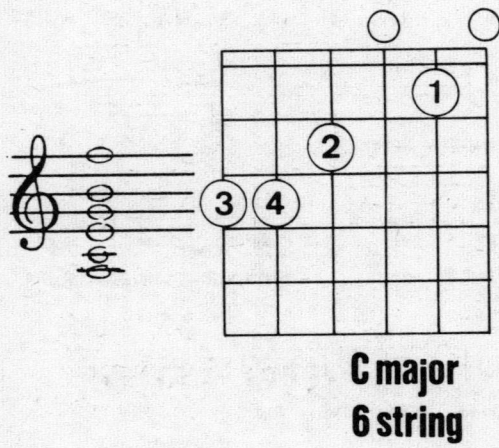

**C major
6 string**

In this chord your 1st and 2nd fingers go in the same position as before, on the 2nd and 4th strings, but now we add the 4th finger on the third fret of the 5th string and the 3rd finger on the third fret of the 6th string.

Watch that 3rd and 4th finger and make sure that they are pressing down firmly behind the fret so that the strings are able to give off a clear note. Once you feel you've got the chord right, try moving from it to some of the other chords which you already know, like this:

| |: **C**/// | **D7**/// | **C**/// | **G**/// :| |

The next most important chord in the key is G7, which is very closely related to the G Major you have already learned. In its simple, four string version it is one of the easiest chords to play on the guitar, and looks like this:

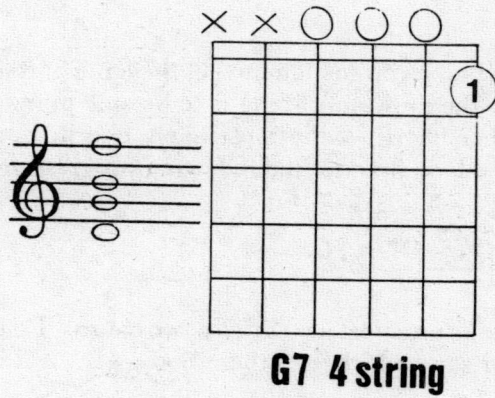

G7 4 string

You're already getting to know quite a few six string chords, so let's try the six string version of G7, which looks very much like the G Major, except that the 1st string is fretted on the **first** fret, not the **third**.

This being so, in order to be able to fret the 5th and 6th strings as required you use the 1st finger on the 1st string this time, and the chord looks like this:

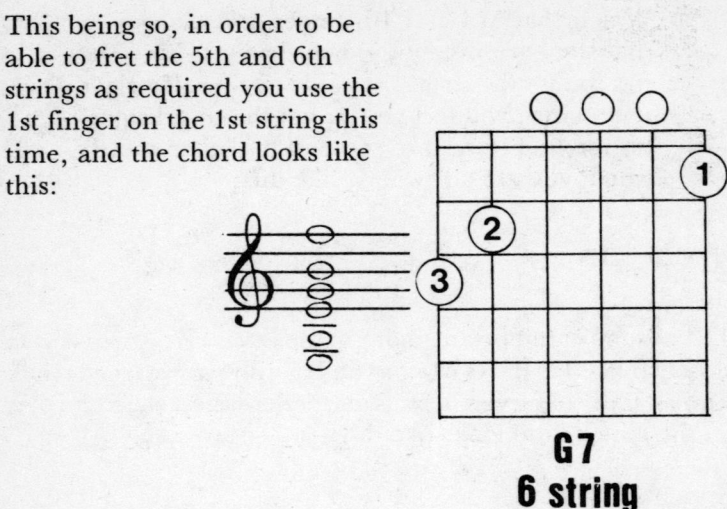

G7
6 string

It shouldn't take you too long to get the hang of this one, but once again the important thing is to be able to move from it onto another chord — the most likely one in this instance being C. So let's practise the following progression:

| |: **G7**/// | **C**/// | **G7**/// | **C**/// :| |

Now, to make practical use of those two chords, I'd like you to try another song which uses them both, *AUNT RHODY*.

AUNT RHODY

This is a good one in which to use alternating bass and down brush strokes with the index finger — remember the idea? Begin the first bar with your thumb hitting the 5th string, then the nail of the first finger down over the top strings.

112

GO TELL AUNT RHO-DY GO TELL AUNT RH-O-DY

GO TELL AUNT RHO-DY THE OLD GREY GOOSE IS DEAD.

The one she's been rearing
                    (repeat 3 times)
To make a feather bed

Chorus

She died last Sunday (repeat 3 times)
With a toothache in her head.

Chorus.

Follow this with the thumb hitting the 6th string and the first finger down across the top strings again. This is the familiar *boom ching boom ching* sound which you have already become used to. Or to put it in guitar notation:

STRING 5   6   5   6

        p   **i**   **p**   **i**   **p**   **i**   **p**   **i**

        brush brush   brush brush

The first note of the song is an E on the second fret of the 4th string, so is the second, and after that comes a D on the open 4th string. It is in a cheerful 4 to the bar rhythm, with the first note in the word *GO* having a length of two beats so that the rhythm goes like this:

   GO   *TELL* *AUNT* *RHO*   *DY.* . . .

um ching   **um**   **ching** **um ching** **um ching**
                                              . . .

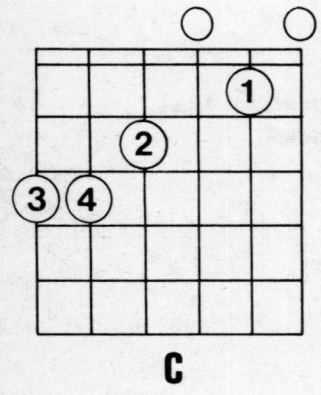

C

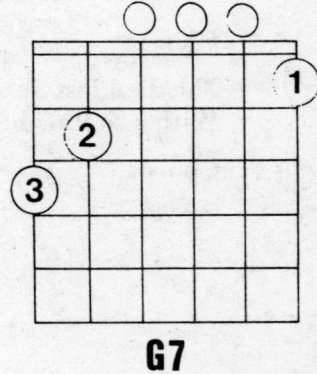

G7

Now for a complete change of mood, a beautiful song using the same two chords, *THE STREETS OF LAREDO*.

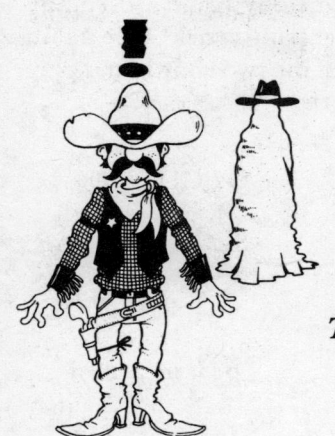

THE STREETS OF LAREDO

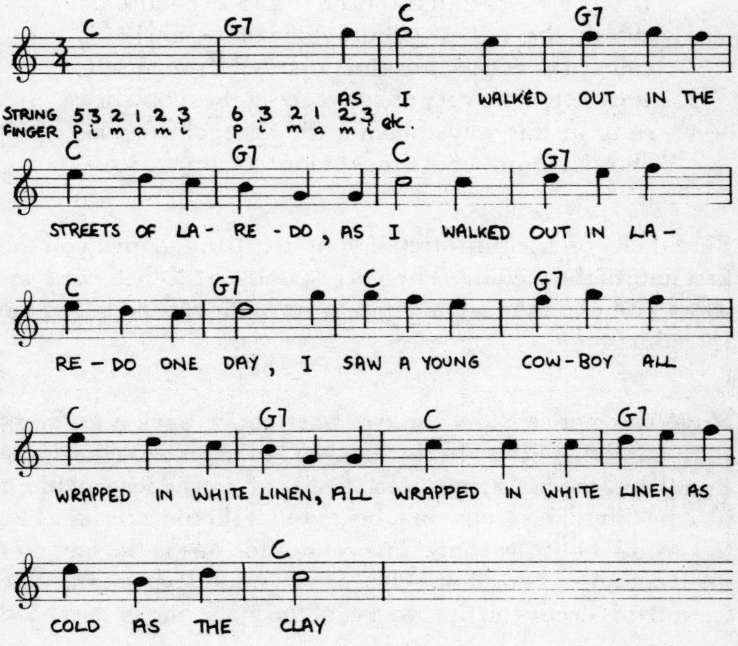

C G7 C G7
AS I WALKED OUT IN THE
STRING 5 3 2 1 2 3 6 3 2 1 2 3 etc.
FINGER p i m a m i p i m a m i
C G7 C G7
STREETS OF LA - RE - DO, AS I WALKED OUT IN LA -
C G7 C G7
RE - DO ONE DAY, I SAW A YOUNG COW - BOY ALL
C G7 C G7
WRAPPED IN WHITE LINEN, ALL WRAPPED IN WHITE LINEN AS
C
COLD AS THE CLAY

In other to accentuate that change of mood I spoke about above, the best way to play *THE STREETS OF LAREDO* is to use an *arpeggio* style, allowing the melody to float dreamily over the moving notes of the accompaniment. Once again you should use the 6 string version of the two chords and play the *arpeggios* with the **pimami** pattern:

	C CHORD		G7 CHORD	
	FIRST	BAR	SECOND	BAR
STRING	5 3 2 1 2 3		6 3 2 1 2 3	
FINGER	**p i m a m i**		**p i m a m i**	
COUNT	1 & 2 & 3 &		1 & 2 & 3 &	

If you play through the First and Second bars shown above they will provide you with what is called a musical 'Introduction' to the song itself. It can often be very effective to set the mood of a song in this way, playing the arpeggios of the chords a number of times before starting to sing.

Find the G on the third fret of your 1st string to give you the first note of the melody. This corresponds to the first word *AS*, which comes on the 5th and 6th beats of the second bar of the Introduction.

Have you noticed that the two bars above have a different right hand fingering? In the first bar, which is a C chord, the thumb hits the 5th string on the first beat, **in the second bar** it hits the 6th string on the first beat, and it should alternate like this throughout the song. The reason for this is the fact that the Root note of the chord C is, as you might expect, the note C, and this occurs on the 3rd fret of the 5th string in the chord played in the first bar. Likewise the Root note of the chord G7 is G, and **this** note appears on the third fret of the 6th string.

If you got the thumb alternation the opposite way round the sound would not be exactly wrong, but it would not be as good as that suggested, because the Root note of a chord is invariably the best note to use with it. **To identify the Root note is a pretty simple operation, because it is that note which appears in the symbol.** That is, the Root of C Major is C, and that of G Major, G, that of D7, D and so on . . .

Now it's time for us to meet the other principal chord in the key of C Major, which is F Major, and looks like this:

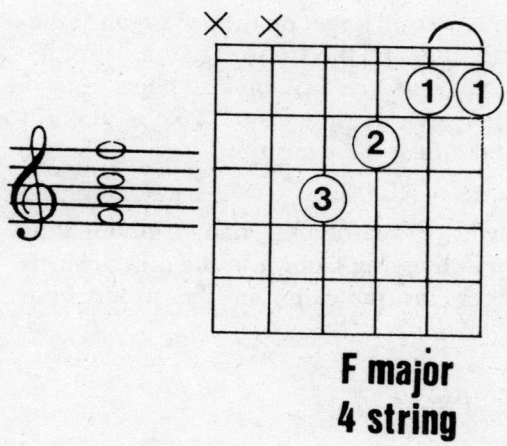

F major
4 string

Looks difficult? Don't panic, it isn't really, and once you're used to it you'll find this shape one of the most useful there is as far as chords are concerned, because it can be used all the way up the fingerboard in different keys.

You will have noticed that both the 1st and 2nd strings are marked 1, indicating that **both** are fretted with the 1st finger. This means that you can't use the tip of your finger, as before.

Instead, the first finger is flattened down to bring its first joint in line with the fingerboard.

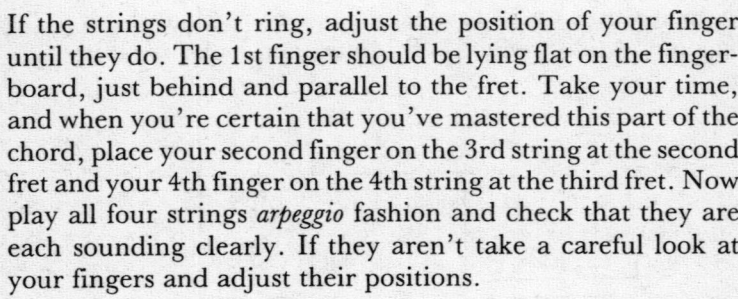

Try this first, picking only the 1st and 2nd strings.

If the strings don't ring, adjust the position of your finger until they do. The 1st finger should be lying flat on the finger-board, just behind and parallel to the fret. Take your time, and when you're certain that you've mastered this part of the chord, place your second finger on the 3rd string at the second fret and your 4th finger on the 4th string at the third fret. Now play all four strings *arpeggio* fashion and check that they are each sounding clearly. If they aren't take a careful look at your fingers and adjust their positions.

When you're reasonably happy about this chord, try changing from it to the other chords in the key, as indicated in the progression below:

| |: **F**/// | **G7**/// | **F**/// | **C**/// :| |

I can't emphasise too strongly how important it is to learn to change quickly, without hesitation, from one chord to another. Each chord you learn is like a building block and has to be learned individually, but to play a chord sequence smoothly it is necessary to go on practising until the left hand fingers move automatically into the correct position on seeing a given symbol. **If you have to think** about where to put each finger when you come across a chord, then that chord needs more practise.

I mentioned earlier on that the F chord shape is one of the most useful, because it can be moved around on the finger-board. We shall go a bit deeper into what are called **Moveable Chord Shapes** later on, but for the moment it might be useful to explore further the idea of stopping more than one string with a single finger. Clearly, as we have six strings to deal with, and only four fingers, this kind of fingering must play a large part in enabling us to use six string chords which do not involve Open string notes — and this must include **most** chords played in positions above the 3rd fret, and a good many of those below it.

The method we use to overcome this particular difficulty is the **Barré**, and this is an extension of the way we used the 1st finger in the F chord shown above. When the finger (usually the 1st) spans up to four strings, we say that it is performing the **Small Barré**, and when it goes across all six, the **Great Barré**.

As an example here is a different A7 from the one you have already learned, which uses the Small Barré:

This chord is fingered as shown:

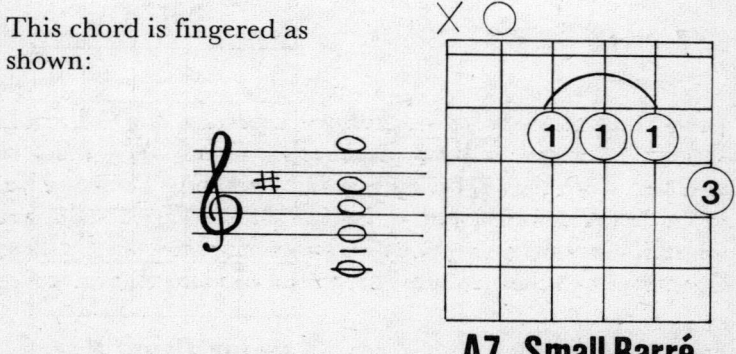

A7 Small Barré

It is essential in playing
this type of chord that
the index finger of the
left hand should
point directly
across the
fingerboard, as
shown above.

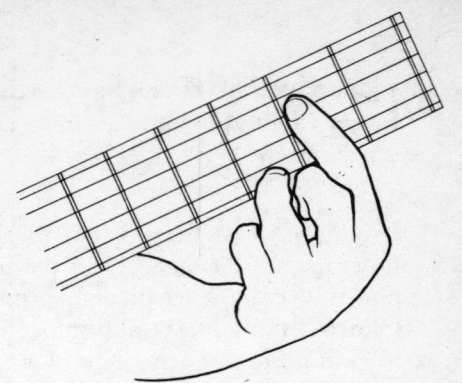

Try fingering this chord. It is highly unlikely that you will be
able to make all four strings ring out clearly on your first
attempt but don't be discouraged by this. **Everyone** makes a
mess of the Barré at the beginning. A great deal of practice
will be necessary before you can be one hundred percent sure
of making every string sound clearly. However, you should
be careful not to over-tire the muscles involved by excessive
practice at any one time. Better to do such practice little and
often, ceasing when you feel signs of strain. This will allow the
muscles to strengthen gradually.

I don't think it would be wise to go too far into
the Great Barré at your present stage of development, but purely as an example let's take a look
at a 6 string version of F Major, using the Great
Barré.

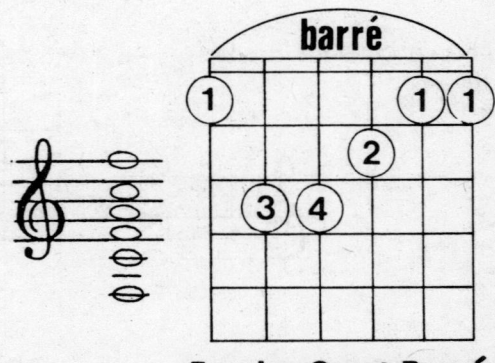

F major Great Barré

The F Major chord shape
looks like this on the
fingerboard:

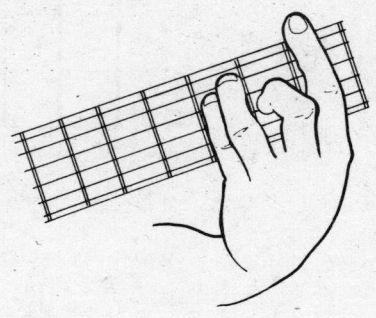

Once again you will note that the 1st finger goes
across the fingerboard parallel to the frets.
Important here yet again is the counterbalancing pressure of the thumb on the back of
the neck. Try it, if you like, but don't worry too
much about practising the Great Barré for now.
There's plenty of time.

Now, using all three of our principal chords in C, let's try
another song, AMAZING GRACE. Here again we're in 3/4
time, so the accompaniment can be played either with an
alternating bass and a three finger pluck on the top strings, in
which case your second bass note of the F Major chord could
be the open A string. In that case you would play a slow 3 in a
bar rhythm, as indicated. Or you could play a six notes to the
bar *arpeggio* accompaniment. You should be getting used to
that kind of finger pattern now, so I'll leave you to work it out
for yourself.

AMAZING GRACE

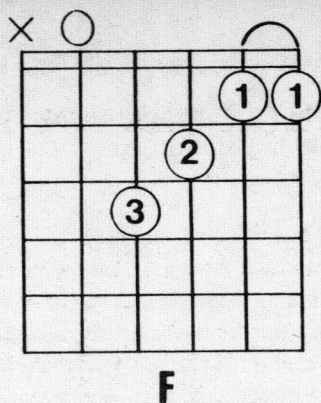

F

AM – AZ –ING GRACE, HOW SWEET THE SOUND, THAT

SAVED A– WRETCH LIKE ME, I– ONCE WAS

LOST BUT NOW I'M FOUND, WAS BLIND BUT NOW I SEE

'Twas grace that taught my heart to fear
And grace my fears relieved
How precious did that grace appear
The hour I first believed.

Through many dangers, toils and snares
I have already come
'Tis grace that brought me safe so far
And grace will lead me home.

TAKING CARE OF YOUR GUITAR

We mentioned earlier about always having your guitar around the house in a convenient place where you can pick it up at any time. The idea is that the more you pick it up, even if only for a few minutes at a time, the more familiar you will become with the instrument. Whatever you do, don't stick it away in its case for weeks at a time and then take it out and expect to be able to play. If you do that you will probably find that you have forgotten most of what you learned and have to start again more or less from the beginning.

On the other hand, even though you may think you are learn-ing slowly, by doing so much practice every day — say half, or even a quarter of an hour — you will be surprised by your own progress after a few weeks. The chords that were hard for you in the beginning will become much easier, your fingers dropping into their correct positions automatically. **But this won't happen if you practise in fits and starts**. I have always tried to impress on students that there is no Golden Key to guitar playing. Learning is a slow, gradual business, and there are no short cuts.

Becoming more familiar with your guitar does not mean that you should not treat it with respect. You must do your best at all times to protect it from extremes of heat and cold, which would affect the wood and strings. And it should go without saying that you must also protect it from damp. Say for instance that you have been playing out of doors one warm evening — something I for one, often do in the summer. Then make sure that you wipe the instrument over carefully when you bring it indoors to remove any trace of moisture.

Another thing you shouldn't do is walk in with your hands covered in dirt and oil and pick up your guitar and start to play it. **Your hands should always be clean when you pick up the guitar**. If they have dirt or grease on them it will inevitably be transferred to the strings and fingerboard of the instrument with bad results. The strings, particularly the thicker ones, can soon be ruined by an accumulation of dirt between their windings which will dampen their vibrations and hence deaden their tone. The deposit of a certain amount of natural oils and perspiration from the fingers is unavoidable during normal playing, but **as soon as you have finished playing the strings should be wiped carefully front and back with a soft duster** to remove any coating before it has time to set.

Even if you do take good care of your strings they will not last forever, despite the advert I saw recently in a local paper: *GUITAR FOR SALE*. **Mint Condition**. *ORIGINAL STRINGS*.

If the windings on the bass strings begin to fray where they have worn against the frets that is a sure sign that they should be replaced. Don't wait until a string breaks and replace one at a time. That way a single string could be on your guitar for years, its tone getting worse all the time. It may also begin to play out of tune.

If a string breaks and you have had the set on for a month or so it is best to replace the lot. I know that may sound extravagant, but it will act as a tonic to the old box and you'll be amazed how bright and clear it sounds suddenly. Normally strings deteriorate gradually, with our ear becoming used to the duller sound. That's why a new set of strings usually makes such a noticeable difference. When you're buying a second hand instrument, bear in mind the message behind the advert quoted above. It is usually best to replace the strings because they have probably been on a long time.

CHANGING YOUR STRINGS

Don't take all the strings off at once! If you begin by removing the 6th string and replacing it, then the 5th, then the 4th and so on, this will be better for the guitar, because the tension between neck and bridge will remain reasonably constant.

AND **better for you**, because the strings remaining on the guitar will make it possible for you to use the Relative Tuning method as you go along, tuning first the Low E string on the fifth fret to the Open 5th string, then the A string on the 5th fret to the Open D string, and so on. In this way each string is brought roughly into tune before replacing the one next to it. If you are in doubt about this refer to the Relative Tuning Diagram in Chapter Five.

ACOUSTIC STEEL STRUNG

Most steel strings will have a ball or metal stud at one end which will either slot into the tailpiece, or in the case of a Pin Bridge instrument fit into a hole in the bridge and be retained there by the replacement of the pin.

Talking about replacing a bridge pin reminds me that these can be pretty reluctant to come out sometimes. Whatever you do, don't be violent in your efforts to remove a pin that behaves in this way. You could so easily damage the finish of your instrument or even the bridge itself. One of my own guitars has a small gash near the bridge to remind me of my own clumsiness in the past.

Try easing the pin gently with your fingers and you'll usually find that it will come free. Only if it absolutely refuses to budge should you resort to any other method. I was fortunate enough to pick up a String winder made of plastic and metal which also has at the other end a kind of two-pronged fork arrangement which can be slipped under reluctant bridge pins and eases them free without any risk of damage. A very useful little gadget. If you can't find one like it you may have to resort to a pair of pliers. If you do, be careful, and don't use the pliers direct onto the pin or you may mark it permanently. Cover it first with your cleaning cloth and then take a careful grip.

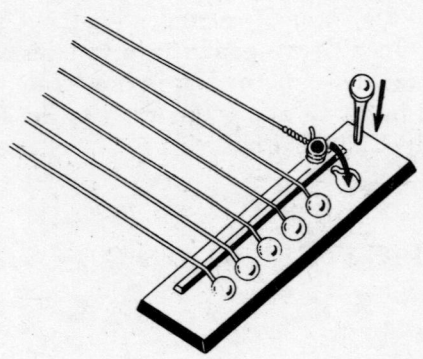

Once the old string is removed, thread the ball end through the hole in the bridge and re-insert the pin, making sure that the string runs through the slot in the pin if it has one. You should then press the pin down, at the same time pulling the loose end of the string to tighten it. The string should then be taken over the nut and threaded through the machine head. After that you begin the gradual process of tightening it up to pitch. Keep your eye on the bridge and press the pin occasionally because it may have a tendency to pop up as the tension of the string increases.

Two points about the machine head end of the string. It is important that a string should be in the correct machine. If you're replacing the strings one at a time, as recommended, that shouldn't present any difficulty. But if two or more strings are removed from the head there's always a chance that you may get it wrong. The other thing is to make sure that the strings are wound on in the correct direction — as indicated in the diagram. There is nothing more frustrating than picking up a guitar to tune it and not knowing which peg to tune for which string, or **even which direction to turn it in**. Pardon me if this all seems obvious to you, but I have encountered these mistakes on several occasions.

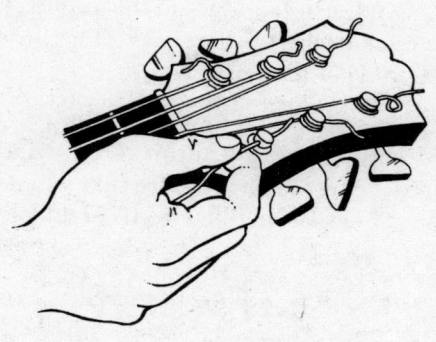

SPANISH NYLON STRUNG

Nylon strings do not have Ball ends. They are tied to the bridge in the manner shown in the diagram. First the string should be passed through the bridge from the soundhole side, then brought back over the bridge and looped underneath itself, as shown. The remaining few centimetres or so should then be wound round the part which passes over the bridge and tightened by pulling the loose end, which is then taken up to the head and threaded through the machine head.

Tying nylon strings to a Spanish bridge

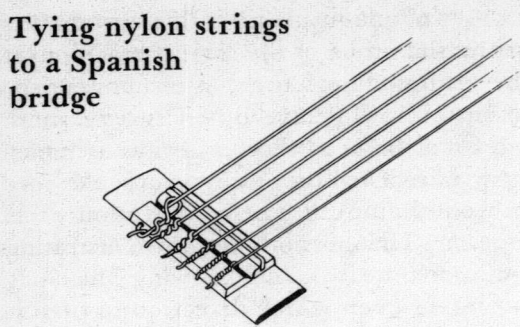

Once again you will have to check as you tighten the string that it is not slipping at the bridge. Ideally it should be held in place by its own tension and to do this it must be nipped in on itself at the back of the bridge block. The un-covered strings in particular have a tendency to slip.

One way of helping to prevent this is to tie a small knot in the end. Covered strings offer more friction when turned over on themselves and are more likely to be stable.

Once again it is important to make sure that the strings go into the right pegs on the machine head, and that they are wound on in the correct direction.

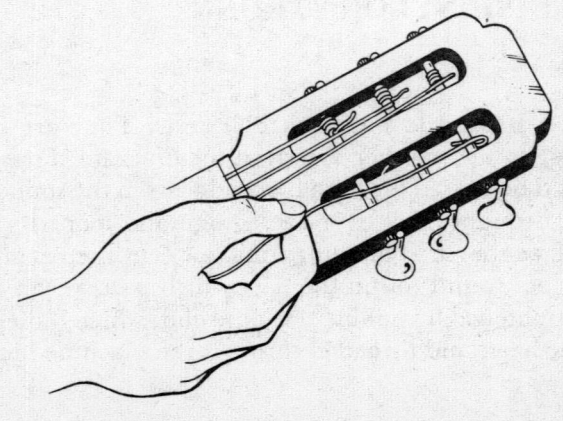

Please bear in mind that tuning is by no means an instantaneous process. Having brought a set of new strings up to pitch you will find that they go out of tune again. This applies particularly to Nylon strings. Check the Relative Tuning several times, and check it again after the instrument has had time to settle down. Steel strings are usually pretty constant once you have them up to pitch, but Nylon can float around all over the place when new, a process which may go on for a couple of days as the strings stretch.

You will find that there is quite a bit of spare string sticking out at the machine head after you have tuned up. Some people like to wind these ends into fancy patterns, others leave them sticking out in all directions like a scarecrow's hairdo. Either of these methods can result in unwanted buzzes and rattles from the head, so I prefer to trim my strings off with a pair of wire cutters about a centimetre from the machine head.

Be careful not to stab your fingers on the needle sharp ends of steel strings!

CHOOSING STRINGS

There are several factors to be taken into account when buying a set of strings for your guitar. Broadly speaking the heavier the gauge of the string the better the tone produced, BUT against that you have to bear in mind that the heavier the string, the greater its tension and the more difficult it will be to play. I have been playing for a very long time and my fingers are fairly tough, so I prefer a Medium gauge string on either Nylon or Steel strung guitar. However, I would agree that at your stage of development ease of playing is even more important than tone, so you should use **light gauge strings** on a steel strung guitar. Nylon strings are looser and easier on the fingers in any case, and Light Gauge Nylon strings are not easily obtainable, so here you may as well stick with Medium.

Most Rock players use Light or even Extra Light strings, not merely because they are easier on the fingers, but because they offer a greater flexibility of pitch, enabling the player to 'bend' the pitch of a note up to at least 1½ tones and to produce an exaggerated vibrato effect when required. These effects are undoubted assets in this type of playing and they are practically **impossible** to perform on heavier strings. A lot of Finger Style Ragtime and Blues, and Folk players also use Light strings, so you'll be in good company.

SHOPPING FOR STRINGS

The first thing to bear in mind is that unless you happen to be lucky enough to have a local music shop run by a first class guitarist or guitar teacher the chances are that the person you're buying strings from will know even less about them than you. This being so, he or she will quite cheerfully sell you **the wrong kind of strings if you don't make sure you get the right ones**.

Bearing in mind that we are talking about £3 to £5 for a set of strings (1982 Prices), this is a subject that is worthy of some thought and study. **I'm not suggesting that you should be mean about strings** — that would be a false economy. BUT do make sure you get what you want.

NYLON STRINGS

You will find these labelled on the packet 'FOR SPANISH GUITAR' or 'FOR CLASSICAL GUITAR'. Mostly they will be classified in Tension rather than Gauge. What you want are preferably 'LOW TENSION', but if not 'MEDIUM TENSION'. These are the equivalent of Light and Medium Gauges.

NEVER, NEVER, NEVER PUT STEEL STRINGS ON A CLASSICAL GUITAR!

STEEL STRINGS

Make sure that the strings you choose are labelled 'FOR ACOUSTIC GUITARS' **and not** 'FOR ELECTRIC GUITARS'. The Electric would usually be **too light**. Most strings these days have their gauges printed on the individual packets, and on the outer wrapper as well.

Lightweight Strings for Acoustic Guitars usually begin with a 1st string Gauge 12, going up to a 6th around 52 or 53 and the best are usually Phosphor Bronze and Steel.

PLAYING IN DIFFERENT KEYS

I hope you will agree with me that we have come a long way together since Page One. You should now be familiar with the principal chords of G Major, D Major and C Major, plus a couple of related Minor chords. You will also have realised that there are many more chords to be learned if you wish to play in different keys from those dealt with in this book.

We shall discuss later some of the books that you can use to develop your playing in this direction, but for now let's learn to make the best use of those chords we already know.

KEY	(TONIC) HOME	DOMINANT	SUB-DOMINANT
G	G	D7	C
D	D	A7	G
C	C	G7	F

The table above shows the Tonic, or Home chord of each of the keys you have already learned along with the other principal chords of the keys, which are the chords that appear most often in songs played in that key. If a song is in the key of G, you can see by reading from left to right that the home chord will be G. The next most likely chord to appear is D7, and the one after that is C. *TEN GREEN BOTTLES* appeared earlier in the key of G, and G, D7 and C were all used to accompany it.

If the same tune were played in the key of D, it would use the chords of D, A7 and G. In the key of C it would use C, G7 and F.

132

TEN GREEN BOTTLES
IN THE KEY OF C

TEN   GREEN   BOT-TLES   HANG-ING   ON   THE   WALL

So, bearing in mind what we have said above, if you come across a tune that you want to accompany, but there is no indication of which chords to use, the first thing to do is to establish a key. Once you have decided on that — say in this instance that it is in G, you can then make a reasonable guess about which chords to play. In a simple song the chances are that the first chord will be the Home chord of the key, i.e. G, and after that you will either change to the Dominant D7, **or** the Sub-Dominant, C. (If you're not sure about these refer to the table above.)

And, almost certainly the **last** chord of the song will be G, **because that is the Home chord**. If the song were in D or C the same probabilities apply. The relationships between the chords are the same, even though they are different chords because the key is different, but you are still dealing with the tonic, Dominant and Sub-Dominant as shown in the table.

133

It isn't easy to find your own accompanying chords at first, but as your ear becomes accustomed through practice you will find that as long as you are able to establish a key, you can play a reasonable accompaniment to a simple melody.

Another use to which you can put the table is to find which chords you should use if you want to sing a song you already know in another key. Perhaps some of the notes are too high for your voice in the original key. If so, changing the key may bring it within your range. To take an example; the first song we learned was *TEN IN THE BED*. This was such a simple song that it only needed one chord, the Home chord of the key — in this instance G, with the melody starting on the note D, found on the open 4th string.

Now, if you wanted to play the **same tune** in the key of D, what would be the correct chord? The solution to this problem can be found by looking at the table and identifying the Home chord of D. In other words, **the chord of D**. And having changed the key in which we are playing we have naturally changed the notes of the song, so that the first note is now A, which is to be found on the 2nd fret of the 3rd string.

To take a more complicated example let's look again at *TEN GREEN BOTTLES*. We know that the chords used in the key of G for this song are G, D7 and C. Now suppose we want to sing it in the key of C.

Referring to the table again we find that the corresponding chords in C are C, G7 and F. This being so, wherever we previously played a G chord we will now play a C instead. D7 will similarly be replaced by G7, and instead of C we play F.

To increase your repertoire you will find it useful to get hold of an indexed note book, like an Address book, and copy into it the chords of songs you come across. I have a book like this which I started many years ago, and it still comes in handy to find the chords of some song which has slipped my memory. Another thing you can do in this book is to pencil in above the original chords the different chords you would use to play the song in another key.

THE CAPO

A simpler, mechanical method of playing in different keys is through the use of a Capo. There are several different types of these, some of which are shown in the illustration. The basic idea of them is that they fit around the neck and press all the strings down behind the chosen fret. This means that in effect the Nut position is moved up the fingerboard, shortening the open string length and thus making any chord containing open strings sound proportionally higher.

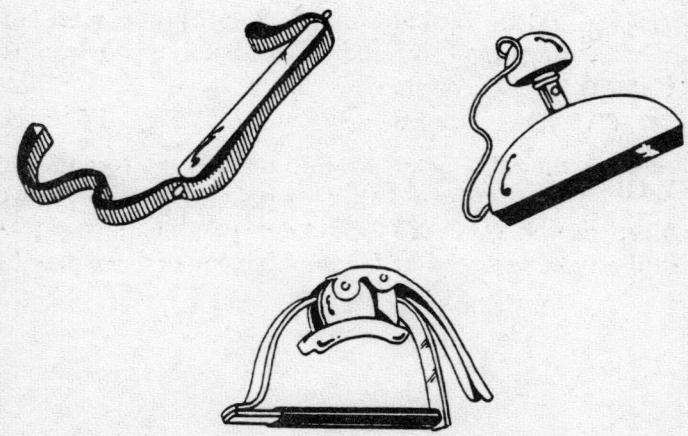

One important note before you rush out and buy a Capo make sure that you get one that is suitable for the fingerboard of your guitar, i.e. curved or flat, as may be the case.

To explain further: if you place a Capo at the 2nd fret and play a C chord shape, the sound you make will in fact be one whole tone higher. This means that although you will be fretting a C chord with your left hand the sound will actually be that of a D.

Don't worry if this seems a bit puzzling and complicated. The important thing is the sound you are making. You can go into the theory of what is happening later on, or not at all, if you wish. In the meantime the chart below will show you the effect putting on a Capo will have when you play chords in those keys you already know. I have only gone as far as the Fifth fret because above that the guitar begins to sound a bit thin and rather unsuitable for song accompaniment.

	OPEN	CAPO 1st	2nd	3rd	4th	5th
KEY OF G (G, D7, C)	G	G#	A	Bb	B	C
KEY OF D (D, A7, G)	D	Eb	E	F	F#	G
KEY OF C (C, G7, F)	C	C#	D	Eb	E	F

WHAT NEXT?

By now you know enough about the guitar to realise that there is much more to learn and many more exciting ways in which to play. You can now accompany a good many songs and you may be quite content with this. But you can achieve much more with regular practice and some thought about your development as a guitarist.

We have deliberately confined ourselves in this book to the study of chords and chord symbols. This is a universal language for using the guitar in popular music, and if you have favourite singers or groups you will no doubt be able to find a book of their songs in any large music shop. This will nearly always use the chord symbol system, and will quite likely contain chord windows similar to those you have learned to use here.

There is a great variety of songs you can learn, depending entirely on your own taste in music and your being able to afford the books. As you play more and more songs you will also learn more chords, of course, and I have listed some of the commoner shapes you are likely to meet at the end of this chapter.

If you wish to go further than merely learning new songs, there are many doors which will open for you if you learn to read music and to adapt it to the guitar. This would enable you to play solo guitar pieces which will make your guitar into a **complete** and self-contained instrument. Rather a good thing for all concerned if, like me, you don't have much of a singing voice!

It may be that you are already learning another musical instrument, in which case a teacher is giving you a thorough grounding in reading music. If this is so you are very lucky, because you will already be some way towards the understanding of guitar music. If you aren't, now that you have come this far with the guitar it would certainly be worth your while to try and find a teacher who can help further your knowledge of musical theory and/or guitar technique.

Don't despair if there isn't a suitable teacher in your area. Many great guitarists, including Segovia himself, found teaching themselves the best method for **them**. If you have worked your way through this book you will probably find other books helpful, including those I have listed below. Another important thing is to take as many opportunities as you can to watch and talk to other guitar players, from beginners to professionals. Any one of them will surely be able to teach you something, because as I said earlier, there are as many styles of guitar playing as there are players and we all have our own particular strengths and weaknesses.

The guitar is an instrument which attracts many people by its sound, and millions share in the pleasure of playing it throughout the world. That's an awful lot of guitarists to swap songs and stories with, so get started now!

On the next two pages are some common chords you will be meeting.

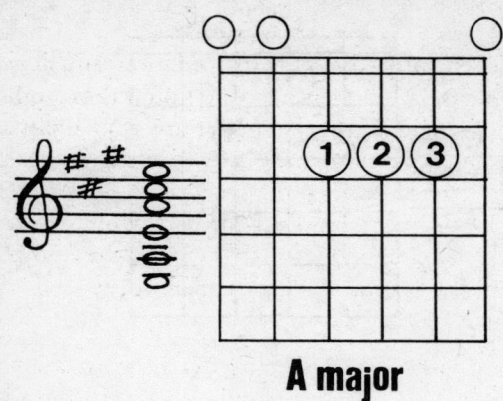

A major

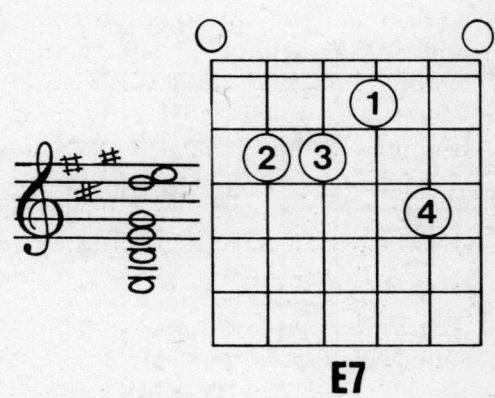

E7

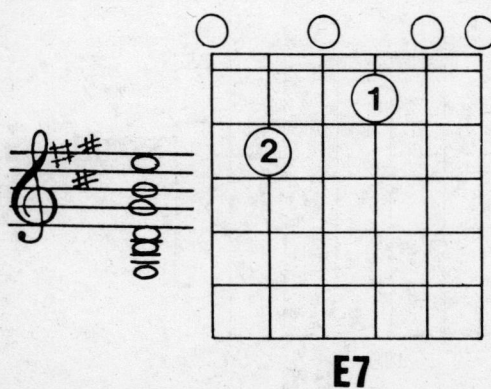

E7

139

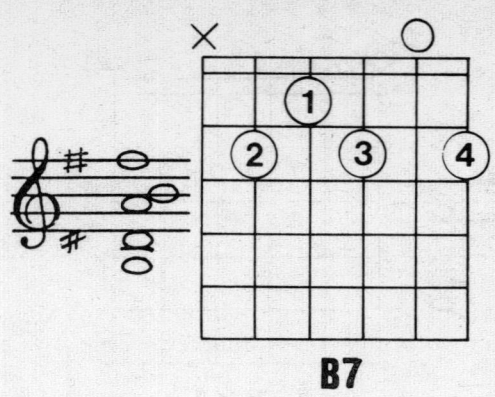

B7

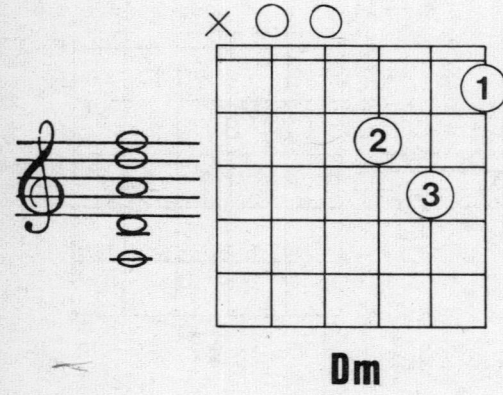

Dm

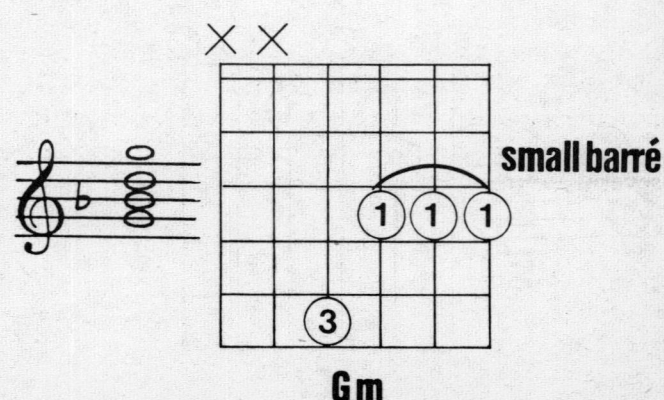

small barré

Gm

GUITAR GREATS

There are many different kinds of guitar playing and many thousands of individual players each of whom has his own particular way of producing music from this most versatile of instruments. The GREATS listed below are listed here because their reputations are based on true musicianship and a body of work which is available on Disc or Tape as a good example of playing in a **particular** field.

CLASSICAL GUITAR

Andre Segovia: Without his lifetime of effort the Classical guitar, as we know it today, would not exist. He has contributed so much as a player, a teacher and publicist of the instrument that it is impossible to over-estimate his importance as the Guitar Giant of the 20th century. Segovia is entirely self-taught – which is almost like saying that he **invented** the modern style of concert guitar playing.

Julian Bream: inspired by the work of Segovia, is another great individualist and perfectionist. He has made many fine recordings both on guitar and lute and has a gruelling schedule of international concerts. His book, written with Tony Palmer, A LIFE ON THE ROAD, provides a valuable insight into the world of a professional musician.

John Williams: began playing the guitar at the age of 7, under the tuition of his father, Len Williams, who founded the London Spanish Guitar Centre. He then became a pupil of Segovia. He is a brilliant technician who has made a large number of recordings. He has moved closer to the Pop music field with his work with the group SKY. He has recorded several albums with Julian Bream.

ROCK AND POP GUITAR

This is a vast field with new players appearing daily. The players below are influential figures.

Eric Clapton: during the 60's the guitar became the most important instrument in pop music, and Eric Clapton emerged as an internationally famous player. He developed the tunes ('licks') of older U.S. Blues guitarists, making use of his own superior technique and improved amplification equipment.

Hank Marvin: many people began to play the guitar after hearing a string of instrumental records he made with THE SHADOWS. Notable for his clear, uncluttered style and clean, undistorted sound.

Les Paul: one of the most durable figures of the U.S. music world, from his trio recordings in the late 40's through his early pioneer work in multi-track recording techniques to the present day.

Mark Knopfler: has a distinctive and recognisable sound and style. He has played with the group DIRE STRAITS and is now developing his music in a number of interesting directions.

JAZZ GUITAR

Barney Kessel: a legend in his own lifetime, he is the complete Jazz guitarist. His playing has a technical brilliance and a swinging percussive quality that make him unique. He is a great teacher and performer.

Django Reinhardt: his recordings with Stefan Grappelli and the Quintet of the Hot Club de France made in the 30's have influenced practically every Jazz guitarist since that time. Playing a non-electric Maccaferri guitar, his technique and improvisatory ideas make his solos seem as fresh as when they were recorded.

Joe Pass: has re-introduced the use of the right-hand fingers in place of the plectrum, and so extending the capabilities of the Electric guitar as an unaccompanied solo instrument and converting it into what is sometimes called a 'lap piano'. In Joe Pass the Jazz guitar has found an innovator whose contribution must be regarded on a similar level to that of Segovia with the Classical guitar.

COUNTRY GUITAR

Chet Atkins: is one of many fine guitarists playing the Nashville type of music. He has developed a style of playing using the fingers of his right hand to produce a continuous bass line beneath his solo, which makes it sound almost as if he were playing two instruments at once. What he is doing, in fact, is a more sophisticated version of the style played by the old Blues and Ragtime players, but he does it so well, and on an Electric guitar, that the effect is truly amazing.

FOLK AND BLUES GUITAR

Stefan Grossman: has done more than anyone to record and popularise the Ragtime and Blues styles of the U.S. Folk music, and he has published several books about it.

Ralph McTell: is a good guitarist with a Ragtime-based style, typical of that used to accompany singing in much contemporary Folk music.

Martin Carthy: developed style sometimes known as 'English' folk guitar. This involves 'open tunings' with a drone effect and an original use of the acoustic guitar's melodic and percussive capabilities.

FLAMENCO GUITAR

Paco de Lucia: probably the finest of the new generation of Spanish Flamenco players with an incredibly clean classical technique.

Paco Penya: another good concert Flamenco player, who has made numerous concert and T.V. appearances.

Pepe Martinez: often plays a concert tour which takes in local music clubs and schools. His playing is very close to the true heart of Flamenco and well-worth listening to.

Try and also listen to:

Jose Feliciano: well-known as a singer and also a versatile and exciting guitarist. He usually plays a nylon-strung guitar and plays Flamenco or Classical or Rock music.

Doc Watson: is a master of the 'flat-picking' style. This involves using a plectrum to play fast tunes more often heard on instruments like the fiddle.

Laurindo Almeida: plays a nylon-strung instrument and moves happily from Classical through Bossa Nova to Jazz.

Jerry Reid: plays in the Chet Atkins' style and has composed a number of first-class solos.

George Benson: pop singer and Jazz/Rock guitarist, he has had a guitar model named after him.

Jimi Hendrix: one of the great names of rock with a strikingly individual style and technique.

Ivor Mairants: one of the great British guitarists, he has written a great deal of first-class instructional material and a large number of original pieces.